# The Divine Woman

Dragon Ladies and Rain Maidens
in T'ang Literature

by Edward H. Schafer

Foreword by Gary Snyder

*North Point Press*
*San Francisco*
*1980*

to Phyllis

# Contents

# Foreword

In the belly of the furnace of creativity is a sexual fire; the flames twine about each other in fear and delight. The same sort of coiling, at a cooler slower pace, is what the life of this planet looks like. The enormous spirals of typhoons, the twists and turns of mountain ranges and gorges, the waves and the deep ocean currents—a dragon-like writhing.

Western civilization has learned much in recent years of its archaic matrifocal roots. Part of that has been the recovery of a deeper sense of what "Muse" means, and the male-female play in our own hearts. Robert Graves' poetic essay, *The White Goddess*, has been pivotal in disclosing the continuity of a muse-magic tradition. The poet/muse relationship is seen from the male side only for we live in cultures, both east and west, which have been dominated by men for several thousand years. Of all males through those patriarchal years, the poets and artists were most apt to go beyond the one-sided masculine ethos and draw power from that other place, which the Chinese would call the Yin side of things. It is likely that men become creative when they touch the woman in themselves, and women become creative when they touch the woman in the man in themselves.

We work with the faint facts of a Neolithic past and the actual facts of a planet-wide interconnected web of living beings. The totality of this biosphere is called by some *Gaia* after the ancient Greek Earth Goddess. It should be no surprise that one singer will be inspired by the heavy breast of a slender girl and another by the wind whipping through a col plastering the cliffs with gleaming rain.

When English-speaking readers first came onto Chinese poetry in translation, about sixty years ago, there was a sigh of relief. It was refreshing to get away from romanticism and symbolism and to step into the cool world of Chinese lyric poetry. Here were cool poems of friendships and journeys, moments of tender thought for wives and children, praise of quiet cottages. There were also the slightly more passionate poems for courtesans and concubines, a minor mode. We were ignorant of the fact that the poems are far more complex and formal in the original than any translation could let us know. Chinese poetry in translation helped us find a way toward a clear secular poetic statement, and the melancholy tone of the T'ang is echoed in the nature elegies of some poets today.

But where are the women? We see nature, but where is the Muse? This book answers that question. The calm male lyric strain in China conceals a wilder thread that goes back to prehistoric times. The Chinese perceived mountains and rivers as numinous; special bends in the rivers, or the contorted strata of high-piercing pinnacles, were seen as spots of greater concentration of *ch'i:* spirit power. Even the rational Confucians of the T'ang era believed that nature was alive, believed in fox-ladies and ghosts. From earliest times, the "Yin"—shady-side, moist, fertile and receptive—was identified as "female." The "Yang"—sunny-side, fertilizing, warming, dry—as "male." And it is written, the Yin and Yang together make the Tao. The fifth century B.C. *Tao Te Ching* is full of the echo of a great Goddess: spirit of the valley, mother of the ten thousand things, marvelous emptiness before being and non-being. The dance of Yin-Yang energies in nature (mist on the mountain peaks, rainbows and rainsqualls, rocky cliffs and swirling streams, tumbling flight of flocks of birds) becomes the image-vocabulary of Chinese erotic poetry.

So we can trace, from the far Chinese past into literate bureaucratic times, the continuing presence of semi-human Goddesses of mountains and streams. They are not meaty, all breasts and hips like the goddesses of India, or athletic like those of Greece. The difference is that the Chinese have not projected a human physical image onto the world but have seen the natural world draw close sometimes and temporarily assume a faint human shape. The Goddess of the Wu mountains, the "Divine Woman," is first seen as a glimmering figure of cloud, mist and light. In the poets' description she has an exquisitely high-class gauzy garb and is heartbreakingly remote. The mountain's name, *Wu,* means "female shaman." Such women were very powerful in the Neolithic and Bronze Age. They survive among the people right down to the present.

The literary evidence for those beginnings comes from the *Ch'u Tz'u,* "Songs of the South," a collection from the old southern kingdom of Ch'u. Some of these poems are shamanistic possession-songs in which both men and women call out for unearthly lovers. These texts are the starting point for the shamanistic thread in Chinese poetry.

As upper-class Chinese culture becomes increasingly male-oriented through history, this strain grows weak and precious. Li Ho is the sole exception. By the T'ang dynasty, the focus of Edward Schafer's study, the lore of the River Goddesses and the Divine Woman is a story of disillusion and inconclusiveness.

The eighth century poet Li Ho is a poet of the wilder muses. He seeks them not only in the wilderness, but also among the sing-song girls of the pleasure barges, floating with lantern and zither in the night. These women were beautifully refined, consciously embodying the archetype, and too expensive for him. They modeled themselves on the archaic images of cloud, rainbow and river. Rainbow: a trope in Chinese poetry for woman's ecstasy.

The Mountain Goddess of the "Nine Songs," part of the *Ch'u Tz'u,* is described as dressed

> In a coat of fig-leaves with a rabbit-floss girdle . . .
> Driving tawny leopards, leading the striped lynxes;
> Her cloak of stone-orchids, her belt of asarum:
> She gathers sweet scents to give to one she loves.
> *translated by David Hawkes*

(Twice on rocky mountain pinnacles, once at seventeen in the Cascades of Washington and again at forty-two in the Daisetsu range of Hokkaido, sitting in a cloud with no view at all, settling back on the boulders in the mist, I found myself inexplicably singing. That song was her.)

Chinese male culture was profoundly ambiguous about nature and women. The best poets were often failed bureaucrats. Their submissive loyal wives were like the cultivated fields; the sing-song girls like the Wilderness. That explains why, finally, in the Chinese prose tales, the Goddess becomes evil. What had earlier been seen as a fulfilling surrender to the spirits of nature became a fear of being pitilessly drained by the ungovernable wild. The Goddess image had turned lethal.

Today Maxine Hong Kingston quotes the folk sayings she heard as a child about daughters: "girls are maggots in the rice," "it is more profitable to raise geese than daughters," "feeding girls is feeding cowbirds." Being Goddesses in civilized times never did real women much real good. She wants to become the woman warrior Hua Mu Lan.

I knock my forehead three times on the ground to Edward Schafer for writing this book. I think again of rain maidens, and remember the water cycle.

The Water Cycle:
The 1.5 billion cubic kilometers of water on the earth are split by photosynthesis and reconstituted by respiration once every two million years or so.
*Scientific American.* The Biosphere (S.F. 1970)

So she moves through us. The work of art has always been to demonstrate and celebrate the interconnectedness: not to make everything "One" but to make the "Many" authentic, to help save it all. Besides being an elegantly written delight, *The Divine Woman* illuminates a lesser known side of Chinese poetic tradition, and is another step toward getting the energies back in balance.

*Gary Snyder*

# The Divine Woman

# Introduction

This book is about permutations. It has to do with changes wrought by early medieval poets and mythographers. It tells how drowned girls became goddesses, and how goddesses became drowned girls. It tells how nymphs, through profanation by the tides of change in literary fashion, became mere women. It has to do with the degradation of images and, at the same time, with the innovation and renovation of metaphors. The transformation of dragon into rainbow, or of rainbow into goddess, was a fact of customary belief in ancient China. But it became secondary to the marvelous transmutations performed by the writers of T'ang.

The book, then, is devoted to a subject exploited in literature rather than to literature as such, or to a particular kind of literature. It is not an essay on critical theory. Rather it attempts to explore the various embodiments of a mythological subject not only in cult but in literature, especially in narrative fiction with its cast of characters, and in lyric poetry, whose most important character is the masked poet himself. Consequently the text tends to drift, sometimes idly, from matters of history and philology to matters of imagery and interpretation. Sometimes it attempts to illuminate the synchronic by means of the diachronic; sometimes it will pause to contemplate the internal workings of a poem in a detached, vaguely "new critical" way; sometimes, rather in the manner advanced by Northrop Frye, it will seize upon an etiolated "archetype" as a principle of coherence. In short, I have no special conceptual axe to grind publicly, and have preferred to take the gentler but more confusing approach of employing whatever probes seemed likely to be fruitful ones in detecting the moods of the goddesses in their many guises. Above all, I should not like anyone to think that I regard this study, whatever its faults or merits might be, as in any sense associated with the feeble, uninformed, cozy, fashionable, and in the end trivial expressions of literary piety which are more representative of what falsely passes as "literary criticism" among most contemporary western students of Chinese writing.

The first chapter is introductory and perfunctory. It deals with antiquity, not with medieval times. I do not regard myself as an authority on pre-T'ang literature. Moreover, the argumentation is highly compressed. In consequence, my pronouncements on ancient dragons and the primeval ontology of femininity must be close to *obiter dicta*. I hope that they are somewhat persuasive.

## CH'U TZ'U

An important source of words and ideas about ancient water deities is the *Ch'u tz'u,* an anthology of literary versions of oral songs—especially of shamanistic chants—edited and published at about the beginning of our era.[1] It contains very diverse materials, probably from many hands, and has traditionally been associated with the ancient southern state of Ch'u. Its title, as David Hawkes has rightly pointed out, means simply the "Words of Ch'u." That is, it is a codification of surviving fragments typical of the literary tradition of that culture. Hawkes has paraphrased the title in his translation of the anthology as "The Songs of the South."[2]

### SHAMANKAS

There will be many references to shamans and shamankas, especially the latter, in this book. Shamans are men who have acquired the power to travel in spirit worlds bearing requests and commands to supernatural beings on behalf of human clients, and so they are able to help and heal. Shamankas are female shamans, the dominant Chinese variety. I owe the word to H. R. Ellis Davidson.[3] The Chinese word is *wu (*myu)*. One of the goddesses prominent in this book is "The Divine Woman of Shaman Mountain," or, arbitrarily, "of Shamanka Mountain."

### THE HO RIVER

The great, troublesome river that winds down out of northeastern Tibet through the desert to debouch into the arid Central Plain, the old Chinese homeland, was called Gha Water in medieval times. We know it as Huang Ho or "Yellow Ho," or simply Yellow River. In this book I shall often call it simply "the Ho," with good classical precedent.

## THE KIANG RIVER

Similarly, the great, deep, and splendid river that flows out of Tibet, across the Szechwan plateau, and down through romantic gorges into the green and temperate landscapes of central China was called Kaung Water in early times. It came to be called Ch'ang Kiang or Ch'ang Chiang, that is "Long Kiang," and in very recent times—especially by foreigners—the Yangtze. I shall regularly style it "the Kiang."[4]

## TITLES OF THE GODDESSES

The chief personages of this essay will be ordinarily referred to with stereotyped translations of their conventional Chinese titles. They are:

"The Divine Woman" *(shen nü);* also "The Goddess of Shamanka Mountain" or "of Wu shan."

"God's Child" *(ti tzu).* She is a goddess of the Hsiang River, or one of its twin goddesses. If the latter, she is the younger of the two.

"Hsiang Consort" *(Hsiang fei);* also "Hsiang Fairy" *(Hsiang o);* the goddess or goddesses of the Hsiang River. If twinned, they appear sometimes as "Maiden Bloom" *(nü ying)* and "Fairy Radiance" *(o huang).*

"Lo Divinity" *(Lo shen).* The goddess of the Lo River.

"Han Woman" *(Han nü).* The goddess of the Han River.

GLOSSARIES OF CHINESE EXPRESSIONS

The glossaries of Chinese words and names omit some expressions whose graphs should be obvious to anyone who can read a little Chinese (for example, the characters for "T'ang," or *"Shan hai ching"*) and some where the text provides a translation which should immediately suggest the graphs (for example, Yün-meng, or "Cloud Dream"). Otherwise, I believe them to be reasonably complete.

# 1 Women, Nymphs and Dragons

Your buoyant troops on dimpling ocean tread,
Wafting the moist air from his oozy bed.
AQUATIC NYMPHS! — YOU lead with viewless march
The winged Vapours up the aerial arch,
On each broad cloud a thousand sails expand,
And steer the shadowy treasure o'er the land,
Through vernal skies the gathering drops diffuse,
Plunge in soft rains, or sink in silver dews.

*Erasmus Darwin*
"The Economy of Vegetation"

## WOMEN AND NYMPHS

In the lines of our epigraph, the amazing Dr. Erasmus Darwin presents a poetic allegory of the formation of clouds, rain, snow, hail, and dew. That he should represent the spirits of the multiple natural manifestations of water as female would have seemed entirely natural to the ancient Chinese. Nymphs, naiads, and nereids, however exotic and strange, would have charmed them, and they could easily have found equivalents among their own mist-clad maidens and exalted river queens.

7

Dr. Darwin's purposes were "scientific" in a way that would have been obscure to the Chinese, and so his verses have a very different tone from those of the ancient poet Sung Yü (or whoever wrote the poems attributed to him) and of the medieval poet Li Ho, both of whom wrote intensely about water goddesses in their various manifestations. When Dr. Darwin hypostasized the plants and minerals of the natural world, he chose to represent them in the guise of pagan deities, great and small, their substances hardened by the classical marble of the Renaissance and their contours sharpened by the severe crystal of the Enlightenment. For example, when the good doctor comes to tell how subterranean springs, passing through calcareous earth, supply the "bright treasure" of lime-impregnated water to depleted soils, he writes:

> O pierce, YE NYMPHS! her marble veins, and lead
> Her gushing fountains to the thirsty mead;
> Wide o'er the shining vales, and trickling hills
> Spread the bright treasure in a thousand rills.[1]

Unlike Sung Yü and Li Ho, Dr. Darwin did not infuse his personified elements with a magic glow, but like them he was able to realize believable figures of river goddesses and water maids that dramatized equally the truth about woman's nature and the truth about the water cycle.

In the summer of A.D. 813, the T'ang empire suffered a severe flood. The reigning monarch Li Ch'un, posthumously known as Hsien Tsung, was persuaded that the catastrophe was a result of an excess of the *yin* part of the cosmic duality. Because the imbalance could be corrected, partially at least, by human activity—above all by the actions of the Son of Heaven—on July 21 the sovereign responded by expelling two hundred wagon loads of superfluous women from his palace.[2] Women represented metaphysical water in human form.

Between these two extremes—expelled courtesans and swelling river—lay a host of spiritual beings, female or partly female in aspect but aqueous in nature. These were the nymphs of the Far East who, like the apsarases of India,[3] haunted lakes and rivers. They manifested themselves either happily or destructively, depending upon whim perhaps, as in popular story, or upon the necessary readjustment of the balance of natural forces, as in accepted metaphysics. So these spiritual beings might reveal themselves as the healing guardians of hot springs, as Dr. Darwin's Hygeia in "her sainted wells,"[4] or as the Chinese nymph who haunted the medicinal pools of Mount Li and cured the first ruler of Ch'in of a loathsome disease—and was reported to have become his mistress.[5]

Abstractly, however, women represented to the Chinese the fertile, moist, receptive principle in nature. They appeared in mythology and in literature as visible forms of the moist soil and the watercourses that make it wet. Both were receptive to the blazing, impregnating rays of the masculine sun and the benign influence of the radiant, superincumbent sky. Womankind symbolized the great water cycle that lifted the moisture from seas and lakes, transmuted it into clouds and mists, and spread it fruitfully into the dry soil. Fed by countless freshets and floods after the winter solstice, when the *yin* energy is fullest, the woman earth permitted the softening of the germs of living things hidden within her and awaited the penetrating heat of spring and summer to bring up her crops.

The cosmic expression of the female principle took on many other forms, but these need concern us only briefly here. What the magical Rhinegold was to the devoted Rhine maidens, such was the precious dragon pearl to the spirits of the waters of China. Moreover, the pearl of power stood for the universal relationship between woman and pearl, and between woman and moon. Water goddesses were moon goddesses in some of their phases, or had lunar cognates. Their festivals were love festivals.[6] But a lovely goddess of the moon had developed a cult of her own in early times, and stood apart from the lady spirits of the waters. Still, she and they shared a connection with the pearl, that concreted replica of Oberon's "wat'ry moon." Pearls were solidified lunar essence—and female essence. It was thought that they waxed and waned in fetal form within the oyster in harmony with the menstrual cycle of human females. In form, color, and luminescence they were miniature versions of the moon itself. The moon in turn was the celestial image of woman-kind—congealed water and ice. A woman's tears were both moons and pearls. But, however strong their human and sentimental significance, the cosmic meaning of pearls remained more significant. They were also supernatural tears—the tears of mermaids, that is of female sea dragons or their lesser avatars—and accordingly constitute an important link, both ontological and symbolic, between the worlds of women and dragons, the tidal flows of ocean, and the changeless sky.[7]

SHAMANKAS

An especially privileged kind of being lived ambiguously between the world of human women and the world of water women. This was the shamanka. She was a ghost seer and a god seer. A classical description of her may be found in a pre-Han text, the *Kuo yü*. It says, *inter alia,* that shamankas are persons of exceptionally acute perception who can sense things far and near:

> Their bright sight is capable of shedding light on them; their keen hearing is capable of listening to them. Since this is so, the luminous deities come down to them. If it is to men we call them shamans; if it is to women we call them shamankas.[8]

So defined, the shamans of China fit the universal pattern very well—a pattern well described in a modern account of Tibetan shamans:

> A shaman is someone who passes through a spiritual crisis, in which a vision determines his vocations, thereby acquiring the ability to control conditions of trance and ecstasy. He or she makes conscious use of this for the benefit of the community, travelling in trance to the upper or the under world, accompanied by spirit helpers, there to convey requests to gods or spirits or to force them, sometimes in a very aggressive manner, to adopt a milder attitude towards mankind. Thus the shaman is a conductor of souls, healer, miracle worker and sometimes also priest, but he differs essentially from the priest and other religious functionaries through his technique of ecstasy.[9]

Accordingly, shamans and shamankas are also public oracles, through whose mouth the words of spirits are transmitted. It seems to have been usual in China, as elsewhere, for individual shamans and shamankas to have enjoyed a special relationship with a particular spirit. An example is "The Divinity of the Heaven of Metal," also known as "The Great King of the Heaven of Metal." In the mid-eighth century, a shamanka surnamed Tung had ready access to this god.[10] This kind of specialization was most useful, of course, because anyone who had a supernatural problem would consult such a specialist in preference to a shaman with only vague claims to universal competence.

Chinese shamans, like, for instance, the Yakut shamans of eastern Siberia,[11] had amorous relations with the divine beings they encountered in their trances and mystic voyages. This characteristic was widely adapted to the needs of Chinese erotic poets, who happily paraphrased the attempts of ancient shamans to lure goddesses to their embraces as allegories of idealistic young men or sensitive sovereigns seeking the love of goddesslike women, or even of actual goddesses.

Because shamans had some supernormal access to goddesses, just as did shamankas to gods, they shared the divinity of the goddesses in some degree, even allowing for the fact that their overtures were often frustrated. Hence the divine kings of early antiquity in China were themselves shamans. Their occasional role as scapegoats for the people, however, was often delegated to surrogates who suffered for them, because suffering was required in return for supernatural favors. Similarly, shamankas exercised their charms on male divinities, and so to some extent shared the attributes of goddesses. The literary *locus classicus* of these transitions and analogues is the two rhapsodies on the Kings of Ch'u and the rainbow goddess of Wu shan, "Shamanka Mountain," attributed to Sung Yü. We shall return to them.

Leaving her male counterpart aside for the moment, let us consider briefly the history of the shamanka in China. The earliest available evidence shows that in the society of the Chinese bronze age, the shamanka played a highly important spiritual role. Linguistic facts reveal the intimate interrelationships between the word *wu (\*myu)* "shamanka" and such words as "mother," "dance," "fertility," "egg," and "receptacle." The ancient shamanka, then, was closely related to the fecund mother, to the fertile soil, to the receptive earth. The textual evidence supports these philological associations. In Shang and Chou times, shamankas were regularly employed in the interests of human and natural fertility, above all in bringing rain to parched farmlands—a responsibility they shared with the ancient kings. They were musicians and dancers and oracles. When all of their techniques failed to moisten the soil they were liable, like their male colleagues, to suffer exposure to the blistering sun, or else to be burned as ritual sacrifices to the overwhelming masculine power of heaven.[12] In later times, these expiatory spectacles diminished in frequency, surviving chiefly in symbolic form. But they never completely disappeared. In some reigns, shamankas held official court appointments, to serve as oracles or in other traditional capacities as needed. The T'ang palace, for instance, employed fifteen Lady Shamankas *(wu shih)*, along with diviners of various persuasions, in the office of the Grand Diviner.[13] In other reigns such suspiciously autonomous functionaries were abolished altogether. Indeed, from Han times on, when "Confucian" orthodoxy in cult matters was becoming increasingly important, it was generally considered an act of public morality to demolish the little unorthodox shrines and fanes of the shamanesses who did not enjoy the protection of the court. Sometimes zealous magistrates destroyed them by the thousands during very brief tenures in rural towns. A notable example is that Ti Jen-chieh—in our own century transformed into the sagacious Judge Dee of van Gulik's detective novels—who, after an inspection tour immediately south of the Yangtze in the seventh century, was gratified to report that he had destroyed seventeen hundred unauthorized shrines in that region.[14] Clearly the common man still relied on the unique talents of shamans, despite their persistence in pursuing undignified deities. Even the government might, in a critical time, revert to the practices of remote antiquity and tacitly acknowledge the special powers of shamans. For example, during the great drought of A.D. 814, a courtier recommended the resurrection of ancient procedures to bring rain, including both the manufacture of dragon images of clay and "the exposure of shamankas to the sun."[15] Possibly such events were exceptional, but the activities of shamans among the masses of the people in early medieval times probably owe the little attention they have received to the failure of documentation. What we get in the best literature is an emphasis on the refined offshoots of shamans—the transcendent superbeings *(hsien)* of Taoism. These idealized shamans were analogous to the yogins of India and to the tantric adepts of Buddhism in their unique supernatural powers. But the *hsien* had abandoned the helpful social role of the ancient shamans and, like most Taoists, looked only for their own salvation. However they had not forgotten the archaic techniques of soul projection, and they continued to dream of magic flights to paradises in the sea and air.

Shamankas, then, were not only involved with gods, sometimes in an amorous way, but they also had some of the attributes of divine consorts. They were, in fact, lesser goddesses. Although, in the respectable literature of the post-Han period, the status of shamanesses appeared to have been comparatively low, their fairy natures sometimes show through unambiguously, even in official history. A case in point is a description in "The Book of Chin" of two pretty shamanesses, skilled musicians and magicians, who could dance like elves, make themselves invisible, and converse with ghosts.[16] But if shamanesses had some of the attributes of goddesses, it remains to be shown whether they also had some of the attributes of dragons.

## DRAGONS

The dragons of northern and western Europe, familiar to us as the monster of the Beowulf epic and as the Fafnir of Wagner's operatic romances, were treasure hoarders and fire breathers, resembling their Far Eastern cousins only in their serpentine form. Like Chinese dragons, they had the power of flight, but unlike them they shot about like comets and falling stars—ill omened and frightful.[17] These essentially Germanic evildoers were lurkers in barrows, where they brooded jealously over the gold and garnets buried with the bones of ancient kings. The *Beowulf* dragon was

> He who, burning,     barrows seeks.
> Naked foe dragon,    he flies by night,
> Fire-swathed.[18]

This creature is quite unlike the beneficent, rain-bringing Chinese *lung,* whom we probably misrepresent with the borrowed sobriquet of "dragon." Temperamentally he was closer to the mild and generous fish goddesses of the Mediterranean than to the northern firedrakes. He does, however, have cognates in European folklore, although these have not received the immense publicity accorded the haunters of barrows. For instance:

> In the Alps a dragon inhabits a tarn; if a stone is thrown in, rain will follow, however good the weather may be.[19]

He closely resembles the "Plumet Basilisk" of Marianne Moore, a kingly reptile:

> He runs, he flies, he swims, to get to his basilica—
> 'the ruler of Rivers, Lakes and Seas,
>     invisible or visible,' with clouds to do as bid . . .[20]

Serpents have been associated with water in early belief in most parts of the world. A standard reference on folklore notes the linkage in Babylon, Greece and Mongolia, and among many peoples of Europe, Africa, and America. Accordingly, snakelike spirits are commonly regarded as rain bringers, and the rain serpent often appears to mortals in the form of a rainbow.

So it was among the ancient Persians and in many parts of India. In India, the *nāga* serpent—holy since antiquity—was a rain and water god. For example, the Kulū people call the rainbow *Budhī Nāgin* "old female snake." In this instance, the rainbow is associated not only with serpent deities but with femininity—and indeed snake maidens are common in the tales of the Jātaka.[21] With the importation of Indian beliefs wholesale into China early in our era, these remotely related cousins were partially assimilated to the Chinese *lung*. From the hybrids developed the medieval dragon kings who reigned over the rivers and seas of the medieval Far East. In their great power, their transient benevolence, and their fierceness and energy, these beings show a greater affinity to the raging *chiao (*kău)* dragon, whom we shall meet presently, than they do to the fructifying and usually well-disposed *lung*. Ultimately, in the eighth century, this very masculine and imperial beast who, unlike the old, undifferentiated rain-bringing serpents, regularly assumed completely human shape, was accepted into the official cult among the high gods who must be propitiated with offerings and entertained by barefooted dancers in five-colored garments and lotus-shaped headdresses.[22]

The old un-Indianized *lung*, however, as the linguistic evidence shows, was accustomed to display himself—or herself—as the arch of the rainbow. The following words, some monosyllabic some bisyllabic, appear to be members of an archaic word family whose meaning combined "serpent" with "arch; vault." (I give a simplification of Karlgren's reconstruction for early seventh-century pronunciations, but all must derive from an archaic original close to *KLUNG):

| | |
|---|---|
| *lyong* | "rain serpent; 'dragon'" |
| *ghung* | "rainbow" |
| *kyung* | "bow" |
| *lyung* | "arched; prominent" |
| *k'ung* | "hollow" |
| *lyong* | "hillock" |
| *lyong* | "mound" |
| *lung* | "cage; basket" |
| *k'yung* | "vault; dome" |
| *k'wĕt-lyung* | "cavity" |
| *k'ung-lung* | "hollowed" |
| *lyung-gyung* | "arched; humped" |
| *k'you-lyong* | "hill"[23] |

Other possible cognates could be added to the list, for example *kyung* "house; [later] palace" (that is, hollow space for dwelling).

Our Chinese dragon, then, is bent and curved like a bow and, like the surface of the sky dome itself, hovers over the aerial hemisphere. The dragon in its rainbow form was widely represented in the early art of south and east Asia. It was the *makara* of India which, like its Chinese counterpart in Han decorative art, appears as a rainbow emblem with a monstrous head at each extremity. The Chinese version, with outward facing heads, even influenced the figures assumed by sea and rain dragons in Javanese and Cambodian sculpture of the ninth century.[24]

Sexual ambiguity is characteristic of the rain spirits

of various cultures. Among the African Bushmen, for instance, the destructive thunderheads that breed lightning and hail are masculine, while the soft clouds that shed fertilizing, misty rains are feminine.[25] In the earliest literature of China, however, the colored bow in the sky is an attribute or manifestation of a beautiful rain goddess. Nevertheless, there appears to have been a linguistic distinction between male and female rainbows in early China. Some evidence indicates that *\*ghung* was the male and *\*ngei* was the female. Occasionally both were displayed in the sky together as the bright inner arch and its fainter outer duplicate.[26]

Next to its affinity to water, the most notable feature of the Chinese dragon was its ability to assume many different visible forms. Although in its most obvious and splendid apparition it was a rainbow, its talents were by no means restricted to this. The *Shuo wen* dictionary of the first century of our era characterizes its genius for metamorphosis as follows:

> Senior among the scaled creatures,
> Capable of occultation—capable of illumination,
> Capable of slimness—capable of hugeness,
> Capable of contraction—capable of extension,
> It climbs to the sky at spring's division,
> It plunges in the gulf at fall's division.[27]

The "divisions" of spring and autumn are the two equinoxes. At about the time of the spring equinox, the summer monsoon comes up from the South China Sea. Then the dragon rises into the sky carrying the nimbus clouds with him. In the autumn the rains fade away, and he returns to his hiding place in pond or abyss. His variability reminds us of the changeability of classical sea deities—notably of Proteus, but also of Thetis the Nereid, who assumed a bewildering variety of shapes when seized by the hero Peleus.[28]

Among the *lung*'s fantastic mutations, the reptilian ones were by far the most prominent. A legless serpent was an early prototype, but the lizard style finally became dominant in classical times.[29] Certainly large lizards were sometimes taken to be specimens of fleshly dragons. An example is a creature, identified as a *lung*, that was discovered in Szechwan about the beginning of the ninth century and transmitted to the imperial court in a casket. There it was displayed to the populace. "After being fumigated with smoke it died."[30] This sounds like some strange monitor or iguana that had the bad luck to fall into the hands of Wei Kao, conqueror of the irredentist Tibeto-Burmans on the southwestern frontier. A dragon was the trophy of his glorious victory.

The most conspicuous lizards of China were its alligators and crocodiles. It had been observed that these reptiles, like turtles and many snakes, deposit their eggs in the ground, but the relation between the depositor and the hatched was not always clearly observed. In consequence, it was readily believed that the eggs of crocodilians might yield alligators, tortoises, fish—or even the deadly *chiao* dragons, which I shall call "krakens."[31] The mortal manifestations of the dragon have been noted in our own world too. Consider the fantastic poet Thomas Lovell Beddoes on "A Crocodile":

Hard by the lilied Nile I saw
A duskish river dragon stretched along,
The brown habergeon of his limbs enamelled
With sanguine almandines and rainy pearl.

To the early Chinese, the alligator was the best known of the saurian tribe. It lurked in the muddy banks of the central rivers and lakes, emerging and bellowing in the springtime—a visible and audible dragon rising to summon the monsoon rains.[32]

But dragons did not disdain to take on the semblances of lowlier forms of aquatic life. Carp shape might conceal dragon soul. Poets in particular liked to speculate on such philosophical matters. P'i Jih-hsiu, that elegant stylist of the ninth century, wrote an "Ode to a Crab":

> Long before I travelled the watchet sea I knew your name.
> You have bones—grown outside your flesh.
> Say nothing of mindless fear of thunder and lightning!
> There, in the abode of the sea dragon king,
>     may you sidle![33]

The crab is armored against the cold seas, not only by his horny shell but by the great dragon who rules it and in whose domain he crawls about safely: he is himself a miniature dragon.

Above the shell-covered sea dwellers was the finny tribe. In the poem which follows, Li Ch'ün-yü—another ninth-century master—exhorts a fish that he has just released into the water to swim away rapidly, like the dragon it is, far out into the sea where it will not be tempted to its destruction by the lures of mankind. It is a bit of allegory:

> Seek soon to become a dragon, then depart!
> Do not swim idly in the River and Lakes!
> You should know that under the fragrant sop,
> To slash your mouth, there is a large hook.[34]

A dragon might even assume the shape of an inanimate thing—in particular a sword of power, of the kind that brings its owner to kingship. The most famous example is the pair of swords given to Chang Hua, the wise man of the Chin dynasty; those swords changed into dragons.[35] A similar tale is told in the Chinese annals of a slave who founded an early dynasty in Champa. He pulled a pair of magic carp out of a mountain stream. These dragon carp turned into iron, and he forged them into a pair of conquering falchions.[36]

Any creature endowed with exceptional spiritual powers could appear to the world as a dragon. In the book *Pao p'u tzu,* that useful compendium of early Taoist belief, it is stated that the transcendent beings honored in its doctrine—the *hsien*—sometimes assumed a scaly body and a snaky head, just as they sometimes took on the form of a bird and were clothed in feathers.[37] But the two shapings are not very disparate: dragons fly through the air like birds. Still, were these supermen actually dragons, or did they only seem to be? The essence of dragon nature is mutability of form, and so the question is meaningless.

Other than as alligators and other lizards, serpentine dragons were most often observed as strange celestial apparitions. We have already noted the archaic figure of the rainbow dragon. But other strange lights in the sky might seem to be the rain lords' fleeting shapes—the aurora borealis, flashes of lightning, odd luminous mists, and other unpredictable phenomena. A pre-T'ang tale tells of a young woman who, while washing clothes, was enveloped by a white mist. She became pregnant. Out of shame she committed suicide, but her slave released two dragonlets from her body by Caesarian section, and her grave was visited regularly by a dragon.[38] This lucky-unlucky woman had been embraced by the same kind of being that had embraced many Chinese queens to make them mothers of kings. Such dragon lovers were themselves kings, by virtue of their power over rain and fertility, like the ancient rulers of the Middle Kingdom.

Strangely, rainbow dragons were not always emblems of good fortune, especially among the omen readers who interpreted meteorological events for their political meaning. This evil meaning was most often attached to the "white rainbows," which were often seen at night. If the latter were halos around the moon (or an occasional aurora?), the ones seen by day may have been aureoles of the kind we sometimes notice around the sun when it is looked at through fog, mist, or haze. Such an apparition was reported when, in A.D. 712, Chinese troops were about to invade the territory of a Manchurian nation: "There was a white rainbow which lowered its head to the gateway of the army [camp]. The omen is: 'Blood shall flow beneath it.'"[39] This rainbow with a dragon head suggests the old *makara* dragons of Han pictorial art. Wang Yen-chün—the paranoid ruler of the secessionist state of Min in Fukien—saw a red rainbow dragon in his room shortly before his assassination in 935. The rainbow spirit appeared in the Min palace again in the summer of 938, during the reign of his successor Wang Chi-p'eng. A shaman interpreted the apparition as ominous of treason within the royal family.[40] These ill-omened mists and auras are very different from the farm-fertilizing rain dragons. The former represented the female *yin* essence at its worst, when it had taken precedence over the male and showed its power in ugly and terrifying ways. In Han times, the rainbow was already a "wanton and depraved" phenomenon. Its omen was: "the wife mounts the husband: a manifestation of *yin* dominating *yang*."[41] Female essence was a curse.

Few men doubted the reality and power of dragons. The opinion of a notorious skeptic who believed in their reality but doubted their power deserves notice. This unbeliever was Wan Ch'ung who, in the first century A.D., wrote his great but unorthodox—and therefore unpopular—collection of critical essays on the beliefs of his contemporaries. In this book, which has yet to gain the honor it deserves as a true classic, he included a chapter on dragons. In it he reports that wise and stupid men alike in his time believed that dragons lurked in buildings and trees. When lightning, a sign or summons from heaven, strikes one of these temporary habitations, the divine creature is liberated and mounts the sky with the sound of thunder. Wang Ch'ung rejected this universal Han belief and insisted on the truth of the more primitive idea that dragons are born and bred in the water, and indeed have no significant connection with heaven at all. He quotes ancient sources to show that their habitat is purely terrestrial, even though aqueous. "Both kraken and dragon habitually stay in the waters of the abyss . . . they are therefore akin to fish and turtles." It follows that they cannot possibly ascend to heaven. Presumably there is an occasional divine dragon, just as there are some divine tortoises. But all supernatural beings, in whatever shape, have wonderful powers, among

which is the power of flight—a talent by no means restricted to especially gifted dragons. Indeed, he wrote,
ancient texts indicate that, in the distant past, ordinary
dragons had been captured and tamed—even eaten.
They were, in short, unexceptional mortal creatures
with an innate gift for concealing themselves—no
more remarkable than a parrot's talent for speaking.[42]
Although, through the application of common sense
and reliance on ancient records, Wang Ch'ung had
been led to doubt the divinity of most dragons, the
same criteria also led him to a mistaken view of their
reality and history. It mattered little, because no one
believed him, and the popular myths persisted on all
levels of society.

## KRAKENS

Transient notice has been taken of a dreadful kind of
dragon, no rainmaker to be praised or propitiated,
called *chiao (*kău)*. I have styled it "kraken." These
serpentine draculas, thirsting for human blood, remained more or less anonymous lurkers in the waters
of north China until they achieved a sort of distinction
in early medieval times. Then, in the short stories of
the T'ang, they learned to assume human guises for
their own inhuman purposes. The discussion of this
literary stage of their evolution belongs properly to a
later place in this essay and shall accordingly be post-
poned. Here, where we are chiefly concerned with
dragon-to-woman relationships, it will be appropriate
to pay some attention to the subspecies only in a special role—that of the kraken woman of tropical China,
a very different being from its formidable northern

counterpart. These southern krakens were mermaids or nereids—although apparently both sexes existed—who inhabited the warm water along the shores of the South China Sea. They did not become involved in the popular prose novella.

The word *chiao*, which I am translating "kraken," is clearly cognate to *chiao* "shark," so that these weird ocean dwellers might aptly be styled "shark people." In T'ang times they were frequently identified more closely with another elasmobranch, the ray. It also seems probable that they were sometimes confused with the crocodiles that infested the muddy waters of the coast of Kwangtung.[43] The Chinese lore about these southern krakens seems to have been borrowed from the indigenes of the monsoon coast. The old name of the fearful species of northern dragon was naturally affixed to these alien but equally dangerous monsters, just as alligators and other northern reptiles were regarded as the fleshly forms of *lung* dragons in the old homeland. In the T'ang period, at any rate, these austral krakens lived in underwater palaces, much as did the Indianized dragons of the north. Like them, they gloated over hoards of treasure. But they were not immune to human predation. A southern aborigine named Lei Man, originally a master fisher who aided the Chinese in their attempts to repress his fellow tribesmen and later rose to be a privy councillor, knew the creatures well. He liked to entertain visitors by taking them to a lake which, he said, was the treasurehouse of a kraken. On one occasion he claimed that he could penetrate this hidden domain. Stripping himself naked, he plunged in and soon emerged with a precious utensil.[44] Although this was the lair of an uncommon freshwater kraken in pagan territory far south of the Yangtze, it had the attributes of the home of an oceanic shark kraken.

The most valuable treasures of the krakens of the south, however, were pearls and golden pongees. The fine pearls produced from the coastal waters of Lingnan in ancient times were the tears of these shark people.[45] The precious pongees that appeared on the Chinese market labeled "kraken silk" seem mostly to have been the cinnamon-colored cloth woven from the byssus of the pinna mussel—the *pinikon* of the Greeks.[46] A white variety woven in these same dragon palaces was said to glitter like frost.[47] The fantastic poet Li Ho invented a splendid pink-patterned variety of the noble textile. He fancied it as worn by the great monarch of Ch'in when, at a banquet, the king imagined himself a god roving the cosmos.[48] It was a suitable garb for a monarch with aspirations for divinity— indeed, a dragon himself.

Some creature of the kraken type—shark or crocodile or other ferocious animal—lent the marrow from its bones to the shops of medieval Chinese druggists. Applied to the face it produced a lovable complexion. It was also useful in facilitating childbirth.[49] It is understandable that the innermost substance of a variety of dragon, ultimately a promoter of fertility, would be useful both in attracting love and easing the production of its fruit.

WOMEN AND DRAGONS

Diviners and metaphysicians saw in many imbalances of nature and weird apparitions the disproportionate presence of the *yin* principle—the principle of darkness, dampness, and submission. Such distortions of the natural harmony revealed themselves in human affairs as the unnatural prominence of women, or the flaunting and arrogance of female power, to the detriment of the established order. Portents of such aberrations commonly took the form of creatures and phenomena ordinarily associated with water or with dragons. So "The Book of T'ang" reports that in 634 "a great snake was seen several times in Lung-yu. Snakes are portents of womankind."[50] Similarly, when, in the summer of 713, a great snake and a large frog with fiery eyes appeared close by a palace hall, the soothsayers noted: "Snakes and frogs are both of the *yin* kind. They have appeared at a hall of the court, which is not their proper place."[51] Another report is even more explicit about the relationship between dragon and woman. It tells that in A.D. 710, upon the death of the sovereign Chung Tsung, Lady Wei, the mother of the late emperor's fourth son, named Li Chung-mao, enthroned the lad and declared herself regent. She was soon overthrown and killed. The hapless Chung-mao was obliged to abdicate. The dynastic history declares, under date of July 9 in that year: "A double rainbow dragon traversed the sky. A rainbow is the quintessence of the constellation *tou* [part of our Sagittarius]. The omen reads: 'King-bearers and Consorts coerce the kingly one by means of their *yin*.'"[52] That is, the rightful heir is dominated by a female regent.

The association between dragons and high-born women was shown in still other ways. For instance, dragons were sometimes emblematic of noble queens.

Here is an example, registered for June 19, 657: "There were five dragons seen at the Spring of the Illustrious Genetrix in Ch'i-chou."[53] ("Illustrious Genetrix" or "Glorious Heir Giver" [*huang hou*] are both possible translations of the title given to the mother of the heir to the throne.)

Ordinary women too might have power over dragons. This was generally conceived as a kind of erotic power. A very old legend tells how the frothy sperm of the guardian dragons of the mythical Hsia dynasty, back at the beginning of time, was kept in a casket in the palace of a Chou dynasty king, many hundreds of years later. This vital essence escaped and congealed in dragon shape, causing panic in the palace of the parvenu king. The regenerated dragons were finally exorcised by the imprecations of naked women— presumably female shamans.[54] But shamankas are hardly ordinary women. Still, women of the simplest sort attracted the warm attentions of dragons. Chinese folk literature abounds in stories, some naively grotesque, some reverent and awe-inspiring, of women who give birth to dragon children.[55] Accounts of abnormal pregnancies among young women who had been bathing or laundering on a riverbank are particularly common. In such places attractive country girls were vulnerable to the advances of water spirits. Suicide, often by drowning, was common among them, but the unfortunate girl was ordinarily honored as a water spirit and acquired a village cult—or else her offspring, if human, became a great hero.[56] In the course of time, the story of a dragon mother might generate new variations. Such was apparently the case with an ancient tale of a woman who found an egg by the riverside. It produced a small, friendly dragon. This miracle was supposed to have taken place in the days of Ch'in Shih Huang Ti. In a ninth-century version, it is a widow who finds *five* dragon eggs and acquires miraculous powers, along with the title "Mother of Dragons." Her cult is still alive.[57] It seems probable that there was an archetypal version of this story in which the woman was no putative mother but actually laid the dragon eggs herself.

The grandest copulations between women and dragons were those that engendered future kings. Such a stupendous affair occurred in the dawn of time when Shun's mother conceived after a visitation by a rainbow dragon.[58] Many later instances are solemnly recorded in the Chinese dynastic histories. Two good examples have to do with rulers of the Wei dynasty, a family of nomadic origin (originally styled "Tabgach") who ruled the north Chinese in the fifth and sixth centuries of our era. They adapted the Chinese myth of the dragon ancestor to their own ancestral legends. The first of these tales tells how a remote ancestor of the dynasty, a steppe-roving hunter, meets a mysterious beauty who announces that she has been divinely ordained as his mate. After the happy union she disappears "like wind and rain." The following year the rain goddess meets the chieftain again in the same place and presents him with an infant son, the destined founder of the dynasty's fortunes.[59] In this tradition, the divine woman, identified by the swirls of blowing rain, finds a human consort. In the other story, which tells of a much later time when the Wei monarchs had established their rule over China, a great lady of the palace dreams that she is pursued by the sun. That luminary finds her cowering beneath her bed. It changes into a dragon and coils around her. From this strange mating came T'o-pa K'o, another monarch of Wei.[60] Here the woman is human, and her mate, despite his transient solar guise, is a divine rain creature. Impregnation by a dragon did not preclude the efficacy of normal sexual relations with His Human Majesty of Wei. Rather it authenticated the divine source of the imperial blood and guaranteed the legitimacy of the young prince. In the Chinese context, confirmation was particularly important in view of the doubtful nomadic origins of the dynasty. The western world, too, knows something of such unions: the god Ammon took the form of a serpent when he visited Olympias, wife of King Philip of Macedon, to make her the mother of Alexander the Great. Similarly, the Roman emperor Augustus was the son of a deity who manifested himself in the form of a serpent. It is said that his mother could never rid herself of the spots left by the creature on her body.[61]

For the T'ang period, we have the ambiguous example of the great Li Shih-min, posthumously titled T'ai Tsung. Although the record does not show that his mother, surnamed Tou, had a love affair with a dragon, a pair of dragons did preside over her parturition.[62] Perhaps this could be construed as a symbolic act of generation.

When virgins were sacrificed to the Nile, they were not simply offerings of edible flesh but brides of the river god. The belief in the necessity and efficacy of such holy weddings is worldwide.[63] China was no exception. "From the Shang period to the Later Han there must be hundreds of references to the sacrifice of animals, objects, or humans by throwing or sinking them in the water (a custom still to be observed in the English superstition of throwing pennies into wells)."[64] "Human sacrifice," of the kind that concerns us here, dramatizes the tragic loves of humans and divinities. It is symbolized in the legend of Venus and Adonis, or, very differently, in the death of the brides of Christ. Such survivals as these perpetuate an ancient practice, either reverently in ritual or quite transformed in literature.

Offerings to the spirit of the Yellow River can be traced back to Shang times. In the oracle bone inscriptions, they consisted at least of animals and valuable utensils. But among these primitive and fragmentary documents there has not yet been found any evidence of the sacrifice of women, or any description of the god himself. He emerges more plainly in late Chou times, in the two books *Chuang tzu* and *Ch'u tz'u* as "Sire of the Ho" *(Ho po)*. It is surprising to find a northern and male deity so prominent in texts with strong southern affinities.[65] The southerners preferred goddesses in their rivers. Perhaps these references show northern influence in the south. At any rate, the Sire of the Ho usually assumed the form of a fish, or of a soft-shelled turtle, but sometimes he displayed human attributes.[66] The god dwelt in a splendid palace, constructed of fish scales and cowrie shells, surrounded by a court of shimmering water creatures.[67] Hans Christian Andersen gave us its western counterpart:

> From the deepest spot in the ocean rises the palace of the sea king. Its walls are made of coral and its high pointed

windows of the clearest amber, but the roof is made of
mussel shells that open and shut with the tide. This is a
wonderful sight to see, for every shell holds glistening
pearls, any of which would be the pride of a queen's
crown.[68]

Except for the amber, a rare and exotic substance in
China, this picture would have satisfied the most
exacting Chinese imagination as a true account of the
home of the mighty king of the Yellow River.

The god of the Ho was given a human wife annually
to share his glittering abode. Like Andromeda, she was
a sacrifice to a reptilian water spirit,[69] but unlike that
maiden there was no human hero to rescue her—
unless we except the celebrated Hsi-men Pao, who is
credited with abolition of the ancient ritual *in toto*.
The Chinese brides of the river were floated out, under
careful shamanistic guidance, to descend in their wedding beds to the embrace of the finny god.[70] The venerable cult and legends of the Sire of Ho return us to
the theme of the drowned woman, sometimes drag-
on-raped, who became the goddess of a lake or river.
Whether honored bride or unhappy suicide, she gave
herself to the element whose nature she shared and so
came to reign in a palace of shell and coral, attended by
obsequious turtles and trains of shining fish. Thence
she might come to the aid of men who traveled by
water or persons who had acted benevolently to her or
to her kin. She has her western counterpart in the
maiden Sabrina, elegantly represented in Milton's
*Comus*. A suicide by drowning, the girl was borne by
water nymphs to the hall of King Nereus, where she

". . . underwent a quick immortal change, / / Made Goddess of this river." Her devotees addressed her in this manner:

> Sabrina fair,
>     Listen where thou art sitting
> Under the glassy, cool, translucent wave,
>     In twisted braids of lilies knitting
> The loose train of thy amber-dropping hair;
>     Listen for dear honor's sake,
> Goddess of the silver lake,
>     Listen and save!

The Lady of the Severn may not have been a dragon-apparent, but she possessed all the attributes commonly ascribed to her submerged Chinese sisters.

In the single case of the god of the Yellow River, then, we have a reversal of what seems to have been the general rule. The woman has become the ephemeral spouse of a powerful male deity, who has usurped the ancient role of female water spirits and river guardians. A naiad has been displaced by a triton, swimming up, as it were, from the salty estuaries of the Ho. The later invasion of the domains of the goddesses by partly Indianized dragon kings had a precedent in him.

Beyond mere metaphysical principle and religious power, and even beyond all too human intimacies with dragons, it was possible for real human women, and goddesses too, to become visibly reptilian—as scaly as the inhuman dragons with which they sometimes consorted: "Blue Nereid-forms arrayed in shining scales."[71] These manifestations need not be transient, latent or figurative apparitions, such as serpents or rainbows, but as dragons proper. The records of such epiphanies are very old. An unpleasant example occurs under the date of 551 B.C. in the *Tso chuan*. The tale tells of a mother jealous of the beauty of her son's wife. She has a good reason for keeping the two apart:

> It is sure that dragons and serpents are born in the depths of mountains and in the great lakes. *That* one's beauty is such that I fear she is a dragon or serpent who will bring disaster on you.[72]

We shall see a number of more elegant T'ang examples of such double nature later.

Occasionally a *furry* creature of the river was the vehicle of a divine woman. She was a nymph in otter form, and accordingly classified by the Chinese among the "water tribes," along with fishes and the like, in the tenth-century anthology *T'ai p'ing kuang chi*.[73] Habitat and supernatural affiliation were more important than morphology. Her hidden identity, as that of other water witches, was frequently detected by a shamanka.

The ideal dragon woman appeared also, as was to be expected, in poetry. An instance is a stanza by the tenth-century poet prelate Kuan-hsiu, who wrote of a fairylike rainbow maiden: "The lovely person is like a roving dragon."[74] It is not always easy to say whether such figures are metaphors or true survivals from primitive religion. The edges between poetry and belief are blurred, as they are elsewhere in the ancient world. The Libyan snake goddess Lamia was toughened into a fiend thirsting for the blood of children in Greek mythology[75] and was softened into a lovely bewitched maiden by John Keats. Unfortunately, the forms of these strange female beings have not survived in Chinese art. If we can believe the catalogues of paintings that have come down to us from medieval times, the painters of those centuries were much more interested in edifying depictions of mutating goddesses. Indeed, I find no record at all for the T'ang period that such a painting existed. Even more— painted representations of any sort of goddess, other than Buddhist divinities, seem to have been rare. However, shortly after the fall of T'ang, the painter Wang Ch'i-han—who served the rulers of Southern T'ang and later those of Sung—composed a picture of "A Dragon Woman" which survived to be gathered into the famous collection of Sung Hui Tsung.[76] But no icon of her fantastic lineaments remains in our era. She lives now only as a dream evoked by poetry and classical prose.

To sum up: the Chinese dragon shares, with many supernatural snakes of the western word, its serpentine shape as well as the attributes of rain bringer and woman nature. The scaly sisters of the Indian snake girls and the lamias of Europe wriggle abundantly through the pages of early Far Eastern literature. In China, dragon essence is woman essence. The connection is through the mysterious powers of the fertilizing rain, and its extensions in running streams, lakes, and marshes. In common belief as in literature, the dark, wet side of nature showed itself alternately in women and in dragons. The great water deities of Chinese antiquity were therefore snake queens and dragon ladies: they were avatars of dragons precisely because they were equally spirits of the meres and mists and nimbus clouds. Despite their natural affinity to women, drag-

ons appear in many tales as fertilizing males and sometimes as powerful dragon-kings. But these too were
part of the rain cycle. The women (goddesses, human
lasses, shamankas) were the repositories of moisture—the cool, receptive loam, or the lake or marsh;
the virile dragons were the active, falling rain. Both
were manifestations of the infinite transmutations of
the water principle. The masculinity of some medieval
dragons is probably also due to Indian influence.
Doubtless in early antiquity the sex of dragons was
ambiguous and variable, with the *yin* and feminine attributes dominant. In medieval literature, the *yang*
and masculine attributes come somewhat to the fore,
although they never quite submerge the ancient core of
*yin*.


NÜ KUA

One prestigious lamia outlived the suppression or secularization of the archaic serpent women of China.
This was Nü Kua. That powerful goddess was commonly represented as half serpent, half woman. Orthodox belief, from Han times on, found difficulties in
reconciling this zoomorphic deity with the ideal but
artificial hero or heroine to which her name was finally
applied, in accordance with the new "Confucian" in-
sistence on euhemerization. Her gradual degradation
from her ancient eminence was partly due to the con-
tempt of some eminent and educated men for animalian gods, and partly to the increasing domination of
masculinity in elite social doctrine. Akin to the
nymphs of Greece, she survived in folk memory. But
her public cult was constantly diminished, and she was

never glamorized in medieval *belles lettres* as were the Divine Woman of Wu shan and the goddess of the Lo River.

Nü Kua, in her traditional form, belongs among the unipeds—deities with a scaly tail in place of forked legs.[77] Mermaids are a familiar example. They occur from China to Gaul in the ancient world. Nü Kua has a close western analogue in Echidna, a beautiful woman above the waist, a serpent below, who was the consort of Typhon, mother of the Sphinx, Chimaera, Hydra, and the Dragon of the Hesperides.[78] She has even stronger resemblances to the Nabataean goddess Atargatis, who in turn had affinities with Aphrodite. Atargatis was a cosmic mother goddess, with power over the fertility of living things, and was represented with the tail of a fish or dolphin. In this form, a grand prototype of the ordinary mermaid, she was worshipped at Ascalon on the coast of Palestine.[79] Nü Kua was no lesser goddess.

Dragon or serpent women seem to have been worshipped as early as the Shang dynasty in China.[80] But there is no way of knowing whether Nü Kua was then already one of their number. She turns up regularly in the texts that survive from the late Chou and the Han, obviously a relic of considerable antiquity, but by then she was being edged out of the predominantly male official cult.[81] Her name presents some interesting possibilities. The *nü* is simply "woman," which did not prevent the euhemerizing Confucian pedagogues of a late age from trying to conceal her femininity under the guise of silk-robed emperor. The second element of her name has a number of apparent cognates:

| *\*kwă* | in Nü Kua |
| *\*kwă* | "snail" |
| *\*wa* | "dimple; depression; water-worn hole" |
| *\*wa* | "covert; hole; hiding place" |

This sounds very much like the name of a snail goddess concealed in her rounded apartment. But consider also the probable cognates of an alternate version of the goddess' name:

| *\*wă* | in Nü Wa; also dialect word for "a beauty" in the lower Yangtze valley |
| *\*wă* | "still pond; puddle; stagnant water" |
| *\*ghwă/wă* | "frog" |

If etymology is significant in this case, it indicates that the matriarch was a spirit of rain pools, represented by the moist, slippery animals which live near them. If so, she is allied to the rain-bringing frogs of the Bahnar tribe of Indochina.[82] She may have been a frog goddess, or perhaps a snail goddess, or perhaps both. In one tradition she is simply a dragon.[83] But in another, familiar in the Han period at least, she is all woman.[84] Like so many other zoomorphic deities, she appears in crude form among the many hybrid, patchwork, and fantastic spirits described in the *Shan hai ching*.[85] Among her colleagues in that old book is the characteristic shape of a thunder god "dragon-bodied and human-headed," who makes the thunder by drumming on his (or her?) belly.[86]

One authority regards Nü Kua as a deified shamaness, that is, a rain dancer, with origins in the Shang period, and also a goddess of rain and fertility.[87] In this version she resembles the Snake Maid of the Hopi Indians, "a personification of underworld life which fertilizes the maize."[88] Nü Kua was also a creatrix, although she achieved no great dignity in post-classical times as a result of that distinguished role. Demiurges and creator deities have not enjoyed much prestige in historic China, although it appears that they may have fared better in early times among the non-Chinese peoples of the south.[89] At any rate, a Han source makes her a personification of the abstract creative force sometimes styled "Transformer of the Myriad Creatures."[90] In her cosmic aspect, she is also the creator of man, although in this role she seems to have been neglected by everyone but a poet, as will appear in due time.[91] Nü Kua was a wind goddess too—the euhemerizing texts give her the clan name *feng* "wind." Accordingly she was the inventor of the classical Chinese wind instrument, the reed organ *(sheng)*.[92]

Although Nü Kua's legend and cult seem originally to have been independent of them, she was attached to or identified with various other supernatural personages in early times. Most prominent was her association with her male twin Fu Hsi—like her, a proto-musician and creator spirit. In Han art he is shown with his snaky torso intertwined with hers. Such divine incestuous pairs are well known among the ethnic minorities of south China, and it is possible that the Chinese versions of them have been contaminated by these exotic legends.[93] They have a western counterpart in the coupled serpents of Mercury's staff, representing Ophion and his female consort.[94] A modern Chinese scholar considers Nü Kua to be a variant form of the ancestral mother of the Hsia "dynasty"; as the goddess of Mount T'u, she seduced Yü, the flood hero.[95] Another modern Chinese authority identifies her with Hsi Ho, the archaic sun goddess.[96] Such tantalizing suggestions remain to be definitely proven, but there is no doubt that the goddess enjoyed a prestige in the earliest periods of Chinese history that attracted other divinities like a magnet. Naturally their identities tended to be merged with hers.

But this, like the myth of universal dragon mothers, proved to be a dead end in Chinese mythology. It was the tenderer figures of rainbow maidens and river sprites that managed to survive, chiefly through the help of upper-class literature.

## THE LAO TZU GODDESS

Now it becomes necessary to look at the ancient water goddesses of China, as preserved in classical literature, ignoring temporarily their possible affinity or identity with dragons. Our premise is that after they became detached from their animalian personalities and figurations—a gradual process well under way shortly before the beginning of the Christian era—they retained more pleasing but equally ancient attributes. They continued to dwell in shining palaces at the bottom of a river or to be swathed in rainbow mists—old dragon associations detached from the germinal dragons.[97]

One beginning is an inquiry into the question of the esoteric religious meaning of the *Lao tzu* book—a task that can only be touched on superficially here, and perhaps temporarily disposed of. Although interpretations of the *Lao tzu* are as variable as its interpreters, it is reasonably plain that the book shows an element of mysticism, which can be interpreted in a traditional way as a kind of abstract union with an ultimate source of being, or in a more personal and fervent way as an ecstatic conjunction with some palpitating deity. Maspero has even suggested that the most important element of Taoism to be found in this archaic rhapsody is its seeming promise that the cosmic union might lead to the supreme goal of all Taoists—immortality.[98] Many different solutions—probably there can never be a single solution—to the mystery have a certain plausibility. Among them, one rather drastic interpretation, which has attracted a certain following, can hardly be overlooked in an essay on water-goddesses. It is well known that the *Lao tzu* text abounds in female imagery. It follows, in the view transmitted here, that the *Tao* is no abstract entity like Spinoza's "God," the ultimate source of real existence, but rather a great mother, an eternal womb from which emerges all of the particular entities that populate this ephemeral world. As the text itself says, "It is the Mother of all under Heaven—I do not know its Name, but I style it 'Way shower' [*tao*]."[99] Part of the imagery which attempts to flesh out this imprecise entity is aqueous, and an inspection of the whole concatenation leads one easily enough to the construction of a primitive, female, all-enveloping ocean of fertility, something like the Babylonian goddess Tiamat.[100] Analogies are also readily made with Ishtar, a mother goddess and "daughter of the ocean stream,"[101] with Isis, a fertility and river goddess, ruler of the Nile's flood,[102] with Aphrodite, with St. Mary of Egypt, whose origin—like that of all the Marys—is pelagic, and with the Virgin Mary herself who, to the Gnostics, was "of the sea."[103] Attractive as this straightforward interpretation of the venerable book may be, the mother-goddess thesis still awaits a thorough, well-documented, and cogent exposition. But conceivably such an inchoate being, not yet ready for full resurrection, is after all the ancestress of all of the water goddesses of China.

## THE DIVINE WOMAN

The most delectable but most deceptive, the most alluring but most unreliable of the old water goddesses was the being who made her home on Wu shan— "Shamanka Mountain"—in the dramatic Yangtze gorges. Although she has always been truly anonymous, different traditions have fixed different epithets on her. One of the commonest is Yao Chi—"Turquoise Courtesan."[104] But despite her anonymity, her personality is more clearly developed than the personalities of the other river and lake goddesses.

The identity of her original mountain home is uncertain, popular tradition and scholarly opinion being at variance on this point. One scholar wishes to fix it near the old capital of the state of Ch'u in Hupei,[105] but the usual view is that the peaks of Shamanka Mountain overlook the swirling Yangtze higher up where it plunges down from Szechwan. According to venerable tradition, its peaks are twelve in number. The T'ang poet Li Tuan wrote of them:

> Shamanka Mountain's twelve peaks
> All placed amidst the cyan void.[106]

In the course of time, all of the twelve sacred summits have acquired names appropriate to an airy-fairy atmosphere and echoing common-place genteel sentiments about the goddess and her surroundings—names such as "Watching Auroral Clouds," "Dawn Clouds," "Gathering of Transcendents," "Pure Altar," "Ascending Dragon," and so on.[107]

From the swirling mists that enveloped the Divine Woman and her mountain, she enticed kings, heroes, and shamans to her embrace. Her literary prototype was the entrancing creature extolled in the two celebrated poems, provided with prose introductions, attributed to Sung Yü who is said to have been a court poet in the ancient state of Ch'u. The two compositions are called "Rhapsody on Kao-t'ang" *(Kao t'ang fu)* and "Rhapsody on the Divine Woman" *(Shen nü fu).* In them she appears as the transient mate of former kings of Ch'u who encountered her in holy places. She never stayed with them, but always returned quickly to her foggy home on Wu shan, leaving them desolate.

In the first of the two rhapsodies, the goddess is shown in her noumenal aspect, as a great creative power of nature. In the second she appears in her phenomenal aspect, as a desirable fairy being—less cosmic, more human. But in both she is a goddess of rain and fertility, revealing herself to human beings as a kind of luminous nimbus or ectoplasm—a shifting misty form in which the colors of the rainbow play. Out of this shimmering aureole the lovely form of the goddess herself would sometimes take shape. The rainbow was, therefore, both her symbol and her quintessential spirit. She was also the ancestress of the royal clan. Fertilized by the sun, she had the power to bear divine kings, to bring rain, and to provide men, animals, and plants with abundant progeny.

In the "Rhapsody on Kao-t'ang," named for a holy hill in Ch'u, a king, posthumously styled "Hsiang," is revealed strolling in the company of Sung Yü. He is amazed to see a misty column rising on Kao-t'ang's eminence—a vapor that constantly wavers and assumes new but inconstant shapes. The king asks the poet, "What is that vapor?" and Sung Yü replies, "It is called 'Cloud of Dawn.'" "To what does 'Cloud of Dawn' refer?" "Once, long ago," says Sung Yü, "a former king strolled at Kao-t'ang." He goes on to tell how that ancient king had once disposed himself lazily for a daytime rest and, in a dream or vision, had seen a woman who addressed him thus: "Your handmaiden is the Woman of Shamanka Mountain, now a visitor at Kao-t'ang. Hearing that you, milord, were strolling at Kao-t'ang, I wished to offer myself to your pillow and mat." The king therefore gave her his favor. She left him with these words: "On the sunlit slope of Shamanka Mountain, at the steep places of the high hill—your handmaiden is 'Dawn Cloud' in the morning, 'Moving Rain' in the evening. Dawn after dawn, evening after evening, below the sunlit platform!" In the morning the king looked for her in vain. Later he raised a temple to her and styled it "Dawn Cloud." Here ends Sung Yü's historical explanation. His companion, the living king, then asks him to compose a rhapsodic poem about the goddess. The poet complies. In his composition he shows her home on Wu shan as a kind of magic mountain, swathed in potent auras. He comments on the mystic powers of the deity herself, embroidering the facets of her beauty, her protean shapes, and her evanescent charms in scintillating language. She appears almost as a meteorological phenomenon, sparkling and trembling, darting and quivering, like a sequence of misty rainbows, but often also like a fleeting bird. During her periods of greatest activity she strikes fear into the hearts of men and beasts alike:

> Even
> Eagle and osprey—
> Goshawk and sparrowhawk—
> Fly aloft
> Or
> Cower in hiding.

Nothing can withstand the might of this tender vision. She also has some of the traits of a dragon:

> Above she belongs to the sky—
> Below she appears in the abyss!

Sung Yü holds out hope to the king that if he makes careful ceremonial preparation he may, like his ancestor, encounter this enchanting and powerful spirit—an experience that will purify his body and soul and bring him incredibly long life.

Undoubtedly, then, the Divine Woman of Shamanka Mountain was an ancient fertility goddess whose ritual mating with a shaman-king was necessary to the well-being of the land. The poet makes her responsible for the generation of the myriad creatures. All phenomena spring from her. She is a literary version of an ancient cosmic myth—a nameless goddess of the formless mists, pregnant with possibilities. She has much in common with the Tao, while also reminding us of that great creatrix Nü Kua.

In the second of the poems, "Rhapsody on the Divine Woman," the author has brought the goddess somewhat closer to earth, without failing to invest her with unearthly glamour. She is simultaneously a sacred vision and an erotic dream. Here again we are shown the king and the poet walking together at a reach named "Dream of Clouds." Again Sung Yü relates the story of Kao-t'ang. That night, after the king retires to bed, he dreams that the goddess comes to him.[108] In the morning he gives an enthusiastic report of his marvelous experience to Sung Yü:

> Her form is without peer!
> Her beauty is without limit!

But, despite her divine allure, she remains unattainable. The poem ends on a disconsolate note. This theme of the sorrow of leave-taking after a romantic encounter sets the tone of all later poems about Wu shan—and indeed the two rhapsodies spawned an enormous progeny of imitations and a host of allusions of greater or less subtlety in medieval verse. In these, with the passage of time, the erotic element became increasingly explicit, the supernatural element less so.

The presence of the classical rainbow goddess of Wu shan—or of a spirit very much like her—has also been detected in the most revered of all books of poetry, "The Canon of Odes." In medieval and early modern times, her presence there has hardly been discernible through the opaque accretions of centuries of respectable "Confucian" commentaries. However, the lamented scholar and poet Wen I-to demonstrated that she does in fact appear in that anthology under the epithet *chi nü* "nubile girl," especially when she is flaunting her charms, taking the sexual initiative, and playing the part of a seductive, all-too-willing maiden. In a number of the odes she displays her charms to entice a lover. She often appears as a sheet of rain or a cloud of morning mist. Whatever her guise, her worship was that normally owed to a clan ancestress and fertility goddess. Her cult was closely associated with the tribal mating rites held each spring in antiquity.[109] Her associations seem to be southern, and it may be that, even if she is not identical with the delicious goddess of the Sung Yü rhapsodies, she is a close cousin who has somehow strayed off into the mythology and poetry of the soberer north. The identity of the divine mistress with the rainbow was still very much alive in Han times, as in such standardized conceits as "a rainbow . . . is also called 'beautiful person.'"[110] This is the opposite face of the coin that, especially in the Han period, represented rainbow spirits as hideous afflictions—abnormal outbreaks of female sexuality.

THE HSIANG CONSORT

Next only to the pastel and gossamer figure of the delicate rainbow goddess— Ishtar becomes Iris—in the affection of Chinese poets was the goddess of the River Hsiang. This, the preeminent river of the south, flowing northward through Hunan to join the central Yangtze and its tangle of lakes, was the domain of a deity of the old state of Ch'u. Because she was, in part at least, a goddess of the Kiang, she was akin to the Divine Woman, but she was not originally a concubine of kings: she was the all-powerful protectress of a great body of water. Her realm included not only the Hsiang but also the wide expanse of Lake Tung-t'ing and the central flow of the mighty Yangtze itself. Her classical version is sketched in two courtly revisions or imitations of shamanistic chants, in which she is wooed by a male shaman, whose luck was rather less than that afforded the King of Ch'u in the two Sung Yü poems.[111]

Her vehicles are two rhapsodic masterpieces of uncertain authorship, despite their traditional association with the honored name of Ch'ü Yüan. They are called "Mistress of the Hsiang" (so I shall translate *Hsiang chün*) and "Lady of the Hsiang" *(Hsiang fu jen)*. They elaborate on an older and presumably southern oral tradition, itself apparently a component of shamanistic practice.[112] They are preserved for us in the miscellany called *Ch'u tz'u,* whose present form derives from a selection edited in the first century B.C.[113]

These glittering word pictures are partly secularized—or were interpreted as of primarily secular significance from Han times on. This feat was achieved by an official policy of euhemerizing ancient texts, by glossing uncomfortably visionary or imaginative writings with thick layers of allegory. The new post-Chou orthodoxy frowned on excesses of religious expression, and so the gods and shamans had to be explained away.

Rightly considered, the three poems of the *Ch'u tz'u* collection that refer to water and fertility goddesses— the *Hsiang chün,* the *Hsiang fu jen* and the *Shan kuei,* all of them in the subdivision entitled "The Nine

Songs"—are shamanistic paeans appealing to the goddesses as potential mistresses. They are the transformed relics of divine courtships, cast in dramatic form. Unhappily, the boundaries between dialogue and stage directions in these deformed libretti remain obscure for the most part.[114] Although in the later, dominant tradition, the first two of these poems refer to different goddesses of the Hsiang River, treated as sisters, the better view now holds both poems to be concerned with the unique goddess of the great river of the south.[115]

In the course of time their legend came to be confounded with that of another divine pair: the Mistress of the Hsiang was said to be also "Fairy Radiance" *(O huang)*, and the Lady of the Hsiang borrowed the style "Maiden Bloom" *(Nü ying)*. In the *Ch'u tz'u* poem named for her, the Lady of the Hsiang is also referred to as "God's Child" *(ti tzu)*. This epithet occurs in the "Canon of Mountains and Seas," which states: "The Mount of Tung-t'ing—god's two daughters dwell there." The lovely ladies were also assimilated to the legend of the great Yao, and it became customary to think that he was the god referred to in the *Shan hai ching*. Thus the Hsiang goddesses became Yao's daughters and married his successor Shun.[116] This synthesis of myths provided the accepted view of medieval times. The T'ang poet Liu Ch'ang-ch'ing, in the preface to a poem called "The Consorts of the Hsiang," conveniently summarizes all of the ancient texts for us, concluding that the "Mistress" (Fairy Radiance) was the older of the two goddesses and therefore Shun's senior wife, while the "Lady" (Maiden Bloom) was the younger and so Shun's junior wife.[117]

In this essay the goddess of the Hsiang River, under whatever name, will retain her antique singularity, except where it becomes necessary to duplicate her in order to take particular account of the opinion of some early Chinese writers that she was not single in form but double.

It has also been proposed that the lady or ladies are not only river, lake, and rain goddesses, but also moon goddesses, and that "Fairy Radiance" *(O huang)* is no other than Ch'ang-o (originally Heng-o), the familiar moon goddess of popular legend.[118] This may well be true, in view of the similarity of their names and of the common female-moon-water association in religion and mythology.

Hidden in the magical, almost bewildering language of the *Hsiang chün* and the *Hsiang fu jen.* we can detect the fossilized ritual of a male shaman sailing his painted boat out on Lake Tung-t'ing, a privileged haunt of the Hsiang Goddess, seeking her company on behalf of his human clients—and doubtless to his own advantage as well. (Elsewhere his vehicle is a dragon, but dragon boats are commonplaces in China.) The language of the poems is awash not only with the waters of the lake and allusions to dragons but also with heaps of flowers and fragrant plants. The shaman seems to have showered the surface of the water about the goddess' palace with petals, and he promises endless gifts of them in the future. All to no avail. Preoccupied elsewhere, it seems, the lady ignores his blandishments.[119] The shaman languishes in frustration.

The third goddess poem in "The Nine Songs," addressed to "The Spirit of the Mountain," is evidently concerned with the divine woman of Wu shan[120]—the same delightful being who is the center of attention in the two great poems attributed to Sung Yü.

The goddesses portrayed in these writings are no misty dream creatures. They resemble, rather, elegant ladies emerging from expensively scented baths. Certainly all of them are vaguely interchangeable. All are eternal water sprites, despite the attempts of sobersided Confucians to link them with pseudohistorical figures, or of later mythographers to make them merely the deified souls of drowned girls.[121]

In attempting to see these poems in a broader context, we cannot go far wrong in following David Hawkes, who has made the Ch'u anthology a kind of private preserve. Hawkes sees the motif of the quest of the goddess as closely related to another common shamanistic theme—that of a magical excursion through the cosmos, the projection of the soul into the realm of the gods. He concludes, however, that the quest theme has been less fertile in later literature than has the cosmic itinerary.[122] He notes the transformation of this weird journey at the hands of such writers as Szu-ma Hsiang-ju into an idealization of a royal progress: the king makes a tour of the world reduced symbolically to the dimensions of the royal hunting park. The whole poetic construct becomes emblematic of the divine authority of the sovereign. His circuit of the carefully plotted divisions of the park, corresponding to the several realms of the world, guarantees his grasp of all creation. To range the microcosm was to obtain magical control over the great universe,[123] just as a disciplined walk through a properly planned garden imitated, symbolized, and could become in fact a walk through paradise.[124] Such panoramic visions in

verse are reminiscent of the ecstatic visions that characterized the dying shamanistic religion. They are
trances become entrancing—the magic of words delighted in for their own sake. The shaman has been
imperceptibly replaced by the king—and even by the
poet.[125]

Further along I shall attempt to demonstrate a case
for medieval manifestations of the poet-shaman, particularly the T'ang poet Li Ho, who identified himself
nostalgically, it seems, with the classical shaman-hero.
An inevitable corollary of such a demonstration would
be that the theme of the goddess quest was not secondary, as Hawkes has suggested, to the cosmic tour as a
source of inspiration in post-Chou literature, but
rather was diverted from the form of the *fu*-rhapsody
to prose tales and to lyric verse. Indeed I am inclined
to interpret the separation of the two themes—the
search for the deity and the journey through the
cosmos—as simply a difference in emphasis, rather
than the sharp thematic dichotomy proposed by
Hawkes. The evocation or vision of the goddess is part
and parcel of the attempt of the wandering soul to find
her in her crystal palace. Both themes, often intertwined, occur repeatedly in the mythologies of the
world: the fantastic journey of a hero and his mystic
marriage to a goddess go back at least to Babylonian
times.[126]

# 2 The Medieval Cult of the Great Water Goddesses

You nymphs, called Naiades, of the windring brooks,
With your sedged crowns and ever harmless looks,
Leave your crisp channels . . .

*Shakespeare*
"The Tempest," IV, 1

The water deities of antiquity got little personal recognition in the state religion of medieval China. The priests of the official cult were the orthodox magistrates, selected by a refined system of examination and inspection that guaranteed fairly well that they would not be innovators in religious practice and that they would not condone mystical and enthusiastic communications with the supernatural world. Indeed it was hoped that they would actively control or even eliminate all manifestations of religious feeling that were not directly controlled by the state. Under such a system, a cult of divine personality could hardly flourish—unless it celebrated the name and public activities of a spirit who, in his mortal days, had been dedicated to the continuation and glorification of the rigid spiritual hierarchy approved by the imperial government, or one who, by prudent posthumous manipulation of the evidence about his character and deeds, could be made to resemble such a paragon of cultural patriotism. But even such respectable spirits as these seldom had cults that extended beyond the limits of their home towns or places of official residence during the period when they carried out the noble acts for which they were later deified.

Confucius became a god. Lao tzu became a god. But they were minor deities, not at all comparable to the great nature gods. Of the spiritual powers who were thought to rule the T'ang universe, and were accordingly adored and placated in officially sanctioned ceremonies, the ancient but nameless gods of Heaven and Earth ranked first, and below them the remote and implacable deities whose homes were in the blazing stars. It is only in the fourth rank in the institutes of the eighth century that we find the most important nature spirits who inhabited the greatest of the mountains, rivers and seas—the deities of the natural framework of T'ang. What concerns us primarily, here, is the status of and worship offered to deities who presided over the waters.

Where are the divinities of the *Ch'u tz'u?* What recognition was offered to the rainbow nymph of Wu shan? We look for them in vain. The spirits of the five sacred mountains and even of a few less eminent heights are recognized: their homes, after all, generate clouds and rain. In the eighth century, at least, a certain amount of protection was afforded them as useful watersheds and as the supports of snowpacks that fed the irrigation ditches of the land.[1] The "Four Conduits" *(szu tu)* was an honorific title bestowed officially on the major rivers that drained the Chinese land. Usually they were designated as the Ho, the Huai, the Kiang, and the Chi, but since antiquity the Huai and the Chi had been disappearing in a maze of canals, swamps, and flooded fields. Nonetheless they enjoyed prestige equal to that of the great mountains. So also did the potent sea gods, particularly the one that ruled over the economically valuable waters of the South Sea, which brought the wealth of nations to T'ang. Just as offerings to sky deities were burned so that their essences might be wafted upward with the smoke from the altar, and offerings to earth were buried in the fertile soil, so the water gods were honored by gifts of honorably inscribed jade tablets and ceremonial silks sunk into their depths.[2] But these great deities not only lack names (official anonymity was a recognized technique for controlling popular deities), they also lack personalities. They were worshipped as we might worship Coal, Electricity, or Atomic Power with lavish gifts of gold incinerated in raging furnaces or dissolved in aqua regia.

On a somewhat lower level, some reverence was given to the lords of the wind, the thunder, and the lightning, but their cults thrived best in the villages of China, where they were easily identified with almost forgotten local heroes or idealized goblins inherited from antiquity and could be—uneasily perhaps—provided with personal names.

Li Lung-chi (posthumously Hsüan Tsung), as part of his many religious reforms and innovations made in the eighth century, gave particular attention to the benefits bestowed on mankind by the numina of the waters. He ranked the Four Conduits with the pseudo-feudal lords—that is, with the great magnates of that age—and urged prayers to them as a precaution against drought.[3] He instituted many other acts on a smaller scale, as when he dispatched one of his officers in charge of ceremonial matters to petition the spirit of the Yellow River—in that context not even styled "Sire of the Ho"—for a seasonable fall of rain,[4] or when he interdicted woodcutting on Mt. Li, whose holy waters had been venerated since antiquity for their healing properties and housed many potent water spirits, well disposed toward mankind.[5] During the reign of Li Lung-chi, the "Sire of the Wind" and the "Master of the Rain," whose good will was beneficial to the economy, received higher honor than they had previously received. The monarch commanded all counties of the realm to erect altars to these divinities, in order that sacrifices appropriate to their more elevated status might be made.[6]

But even when times were conceivably best for the water goddesses, as those golden days should have been, their feminine personalities, which were certainly familiar to the highly literate administrative class, were never allowed to intrude into the language of official documents and officially sanctioned rites. There they were nameless and asexual, or at best were endowed with a certain pallid masculinity by the nature of the lordly or kingly titles sometimes bestowed on them. But most often they were referred to only as abstract entities, as the "Spirit" or "Deity" of whatever physical body they inhabited—the great mountains, rivers, and sea. When Chang Yüeh, the great minister of state, addressed his thankful invocation to "the Deity of the Great Kiang" he gave it no name or further identity, using only the honorific title "king" throughout his address.[7] No hint here of the Wu shan goddess or of the Hsiang goddess, both of whom had venerable claims on major parts of the Kiang in ancient religion and were well remembered in refined medieval literature and in popular lore and tales. Perhaps it is possible to explain some of this by applying the stereotype of "Indian influence." In the case of the God of the South Sea in T'ang times,[8] for instance, we have an influential deity who bore certain resemblances to the nāga-lords of the ocean depths, with infinite resources of pearls and other treasures at their disposal. But I suspect that the Indianization was only a minor factor, superadded to a trend that had been becoming increasingly conspicuous since the end of the Chou period: the masculinization of upper-class life required by official "Confucian" policy. This tended to erase surviving female elements, not only in social life and politics but also in the officially supported religion. The subtle devotions owed the ancient dragon ladies came to be regarded as sinister.

A few traces of the old goddesses can be detected in T'ang unofficial cult and popular lore, but they are so insignificant as to be hardly worth mentioning. Examples follow.

It was said in the T'ang period that the god of Mt. Yai in Shansi took the daughter of the Sire of the Ho to wife. The natives of that region, when oppressed by drought, would set fire to the mountain slopes. Alarmed at the peril in which his daughter stood, the deity of the river would not fail to send a fall of rain.[9] This is good draconic activity, but the role of the female in it is purely passive, and the nymph can hardly be described as the center of a cult.

The T'ang writer Ch'u Szu-tsung provides a fleeting glimpse of a rather more important river goddess. His poem records a visit to the shrine of a "superwoman" *(sheng nü)* in a setting of cool, lichen-spotted cliffs. A river winds around the fane of this Lorelei, and colorful flowers reflected in a deep pool suggest the painted face of a beautiful woman reflected in a mirror. The motif of the bend in a river—especially a place where the water winds through cliffs and mountains—as the habitat of a great goddess is typical, and is associated with the Goddess of Shamanka Gorge in particular.[10] In Ch'u's poem, the goddess comes with "clouds and rain" and departs scented with the perfume of melilot.[11] Though unnamed, she is clearly the prettified relict of a great river deity, showing some of the attributes revealed in the ancient poems in honor of the Wu shan goddess and of the Hsiang goddess. But evidence of this kind hardly suffices to recreate the picture of the rural religious honors given in T'ang times to the ancient goddesses. The T'ang poets were not prone to represent rustic rites in their full crudity. The much-traveled Ts'en Shen, however, has left us a poem with the title of "The Shrine of a Dragon Woman," written after seeing a primitive ceremony in honor of a Szechwanese river deity. It releases slightly more than the usual aroma of ethnic verisimilitude:

The dragon woman—from whence does she come?
But when she comes—she rides the wind and rain!
At the hall of her fane, below the blue woods,
She coils sinuously, as if about to speak to you.
Men of Shu vie there, with worshipful thoughts,
To offer her wine to the beating of drums.[12]

Here the goddess shows herself in dragon form, but the rainbow woman of Wu shan can also be detected in the rain that comes with her, and in the homeland of her worshippers. In short, the fading female water spirits continued to get some recognition from wandering or exiled poets and writers of popular tales, but the aesthetic preoccupations of these men usually led them to avoid descriptions of the details of the rites performed in the ladies' honor and of the extent and influence of their cults. The result is the same as that brought about by official preference for spiritual anonymity: the goddesses tend to become formless ghosts rather than recognizable hieratic powers.

Still, although such ambiguous literary fragments as these tell us little about the forms under which the classical goddesses were actually venerated, their names and shapes can occasionally be detected.

NÜ KUA

Despite her disappearance from the official cult, Nü Kua was well-remembered. A representation of her with a female torso and with her tail intertwined with that of her consort Fu Hsi has been found on a piece of cotton in a T'ang tomb—she was still the old rainbow dragon she had been in antiquity.[13] Her shrines were still honored even though the poets remembered only fragments of her biography. For them she was the repairer of the shattered sky-dome and the molder of men out of the primordial mud, but otherwise she had little place in literature, and the degree of the persistence of her cult in the lower levels of society is in doubt.

It was in toponymy that she really came into her own. Her name appears scattered up and down the landscape of medieval China. She has her mountains, her grottoes, her secret haunts.[14]

A mountain in Kan-chou in modern Kiangsi was noted for its rocky summit that resembled a man-made belvedere. This was known as Nü Kua's Palace, or sometimes as Nü Kua's Stone. The names were several centuries old, and even as late as Southern Sung times it was reported that after a rainstorm a man could hear the sound of ghostly drums beating on the mountain.[15]

Chin-chou, in modern Shensi, a region noted for its limes, musk, and placer gold, had a Nü Kua Mountain.[16] An old barrow that stood somewhere by the Yellow River bore the name "Nü Kua's Tumulus." An eighth-century writer named Ch'iao T'an wrote a pleasant essay on this landmark.[17] It begins:

> I ascend the old Frontier barrier of the Yellow Dragon,
> Look off to the middle flow of the vast Ho:
> There it stands alone, a solitary tor, much drenched
>      but never drowned—
> The Tumulus of Nü Kua!

He goes on to tell that this was still regarded as a holy place in his day. He refers conventionally to the goddess's job of repairing the sky and to her skill at playing the reed organ. He takes note of her intimate relations with the forces of water. At the end he laments that this rather dilapidated mount cannot compare in majesty with such natural memorials as the Mountain of Nine Uncertainties, the burial place of Shun. Very probably this barrow is none other than the "Tomb of Nü Kua." The mysterious disappearance of that tomb under the waters of the Ho received official notice in the T'ang dynastic history. Its location is given as in Kuo-chou (in Honan province) "in the midst of the Yellow Ho." The mound disappeared during a rainstorm in the summer of 752, and emerged again after a thunderstorm on June 29, 759. Diviners gave an ominous interpretation to this event: "When graves and tombs move of themselves, the Subcelestial Realm will be shattered."[18] Indeed the oecumene had already been shattered by the uprising led by An Lu-shan.

An extended version of this story, differing in a number of particulars from the brief official account, has come down to us. The dates differ, and in the longer story there is an actual epiphany of the goddess. It tells that when the son of Li Lung-chi, Li Heng (canonized Su Tsung), was concluding his campaign against the rebellious forces of An Lu-shan and—in view of the expected abdication of his imperial father—was near the point of assuming the purple, he stopped with his troops at a post station in what is now Inner Mongolia. It was dusk. To the astonishment of the soldiers, a large and stately woman appeared at the gateway of the camp, carrying a pair of carp and crying with anguish for the attention of the future sovereign. A lurking trooper was able to see that her arms were covered with scales. But the sky darkened, and she disappeared. Later, when Li Heng, officially en-throned, was in residence in Ch'ang-an, he received a report that in 754 the tomb of Nü Kua in Western Honan had disappeared into the Yellow River during a violent storm. Now, about two years later, with another display of meteorological disturbances, it had burst forth from the water accompanied by two tall willows and a great rock. Pictures of this miracle were transmitted to the court, and the emperor ordered sac-rifices to be offered at the sacred site. In the ninth cen-tury, writes our author, the barrow was still visible to pilgrims. He concludes his tale with the suggestion that the mad woman at the monarch's military head-quarters had indeed been Nü Kua complaining about the submergence of her tumulus. Evidently the acces-sion of Li Heng had magically restored it, signaling an end to the troubles that had put the T'ang empire in danger.[19] This account, written by that indefatigable collector of wonders, Tuan Ch'eng-shih, is partly a stupefying miracle tale of the kind so much admired in the late T'ang period and partly a justification of the ambiguous abdication of Li Lung-chi in favor of his son and his son's partisans. The deceased goddess (for the Chinese, gods could die), scaled like a fish or drag-on (carp are notorious dragon disguises), had ap-pealed to the legitimate Son of Heaven for help. His accession led to a flood of divine energy sufficient to restore her posthumous dignity. In fact, the goddess was far from finally dead, despite the visible presence of her tomb or cenotaph.

## THE DIVINE WOMAN

The rainbow goddess of Wu shan fared somewhat better than Nü Kua among the elite classes of T'ang. The prestige of classical poetry kept her image bright while the forms of many of her wet sisters paled and had disappeared by medieval times. Others were degraded to the status of the daughters of dragon kings in light, fanciful prose. In cult practice, they often degenerated into bucolic kelpies enjoying lowly honors in squalid country shrines. But hardly a poet, good or bad, who visited the Yangtze gorges in T'ang times failed to compose at least one quatrain in honor of the delicate rainbow woman and her temple. They wrote less out of piety than out of polite respect for the traditional glamour of a great figure in ancient literature. So did English poets indite their intellectual or romantic respect for the ruined temples of the gods of Greece and Rome, known to them only from Homer or Ovid. However, it appears that the temple of the Wu shan goddess was, at least periodically, far from ruined, and there are glimmerings of true awe of the supernatural in some of the effusions inspired by the holy place. The total output of T'ang versification on the theme is staggering and beyond reproducing here, but the gifted ninth-century poet Li Ch'ün-yü may serve as an example of a writer who composed prolifically on this subject. He wrote, for instance, two quatrains entitled "An Overnight Stay at the Temple by Shamanka Mountain."[20]

> Forlorn and bleak her high hall: parted from
> the Lord of Ch'u,

That jade person goes up in the sky to chase
    the running clouds.
My boat, moored beneath twelve peaks and tors
Is shrouded and zoned with perfume, still
    smelled at midnight.

Her temple is shut on the spring mountain—
    moon bright at dawn.
Wave sounds turning, blending—trees grizzled green.
Ever since that one parting, in King Hsiang's dream,
Clouds and rain fly vainly where Shaman Gorge extends.

Evidently it was customary for visitors to come to the
shrine by water, and to pay their respects on the shore.
Resting in a boat, a poetical mind could devise fanciful
variations on the ancient theme: the dramatic setting
between forested hills and churning river; the goddess
as a rain spirit and sky treader; the transitory nature of
passionate love; the contrast between miserable lone-
liness and the enchanting, erotic scent that betokens
the presence of the goddess. Many poets treated this
subject, but Ch'ün-yü's words are fairer than most,
handsomely blending his own experience with that of
the divine king. Still, the ninth century was a nostalgic
and fantastic age, when men were preoccupied with
weird tales and fascinated by mysteries. Poets enjoyed
the damp gloom of mountain slopes and the spectral
howling of gibbons. But in a sense the poems about
Wu shan are opaque. They interpose themselves between the reader and the landscape, showing, instead
of stone steps, painted images and rustic worshippers
(if such there were), only divine atmospherics. If the
goddess appears at all, it is as a ghostly hallucination.

It was a favorite device of the poets to detect her presence and even her appearance in the elements of that landscape. In a poem written in the ninth century by Liu Ts'ang, the clouds clot to form her glossy earlocks; the sheets of cold rain become her gauzy dress.[21] Wen T'ing-yün, the celebrated writer of the same period, sees the green eyebrow makeup of a handsome woman in the twelve peaks of Wu shan at daybreak: the goddess shines above the dense blackness of her temple, shaded by climbing figs.[22] The poet also introduces a syncretic theme: a night scene, haunted by the tinkle of girdle ornaments, in a dense grove of tear-spotted bamboos: the goddess has been identified with the Consort of the Hsiang. Similarly, Liu Yü-hsi, in a poem on the goddess's temple at Wu shan with the usual references to the twelve densely wooded peaks, the drifting mists, and the remote King of Ch'u, discovers the fading makeup of a lovely woman in the drooping flowers on the mountainside, while the driving rain carries a touch of her strange perfume.[23] But these picturesque visions of vegetable and meteorological femininity tell us little or nothing of the reflections—let alone the presence—of genuine worshippers at her shrine. We learn that a temple was indeed available to visitors, but I would like to be supplied with a prosy little guide to the shrine and its environs, done by the order of the local magistrate, or better yet, in place of the endless and repetitious raptures, a deceptively plain account by Liu Tsung-yüan of the sort that he produced many times during his last years in exile.

## THE LO DIVINITY

The waters of the Lo River enjoyed a reputation as venerable as those of the great Ho itself, into which it ultimately empties. They appear prominently in the earliest Chinese literature and never lost their nostalgic fascination, which depended finally on the central position of the river in the ancient plains civilization of Shang. In medieval times, the metropolis of Lo-yang, on the banks of the Lo, was still a divine city, and its environs were admired as particularly favored by nature—distinguished by lovely gardens, serene riverbanks, and gentle deities. This pleasant region provided an early foreshadowing of the sweet and warm new lands of the Yangtze valley.

The only goddess whose literary repute was as great as those of the southern goddesses of Wu shan and the Hsiang River was the goddess of the Lo. The antiquity of her cult is not known. Classic tradition, at least, claimed that sacrifice had been made to the spirit of that river in the very earliest times. To be precise where precision is laughable, this happened in the fiftieth year of the reign of the high god and innovator of civilization, Huang Ti, "The Yellow Divinity."[24] There is other ancient evidence of the reverence in which the river was held. But we have no way of knowing whether the river deity was pictured as female in antiquity. By the end of the Chou dynasty, a goddess known as Consort Fu *(Fu fei)* appears.[25] By Han times she was regarded as the spirit of a woman drowned in the Lo River, and so became its protectress. Still later, evidently not before the T'ang period, she was taken to be the daughter of the culture hero Fu Hsi, and indeed his alter ego, much like Nü Kua.[26]

The fame of the Lo Divinity in poetry is rather late. It rests mainly on a popular rhapsodic treatment of her written by Ts'ao Chih in the third century A.D. That work owes much to the style of the ancient Sung Yü poems but lacks almost entirely the sense of reverence that informed them. Ts'ao Chih seems to have regarded the goddess of the Lo merely as a suitable romantic subject for poetic treatment, without feeling the need to commit himself to a view about her holy power or her real existence.[27] In the introduction to his famous pastiche, he tells us that in the year A.D. 222 he was returning home from a formal visit to the court at Lo-Yang. Crossing the Lo River, he recalls the old tradition that the deity of the river is in fact Fu Fei— "Consort Fu." Remembering Sung Yü's account of the divine woman of Ch'u, the poet is moved to write a comparable *fu* on her northern counterpart. In it he tells of meeting a lovely person. He asks the driver of his carriage: "What person is that, who is so ravishingly beautiful?"[28] The charioteer speaks of her in glowing verses, partly reminiscent of Sung Yü's rhapsody:

> As to her form—
> She flutters like a startled swan,
> She twists and turns like a roving dragon.

Her costume is that of a classical queen, and its description is based on an historical record:

> She wears head ornaments of gold and halcyon
> feathers;

And sewn with shining pearls that make her
   torso radiant![29]

The magic pearls and kingfisher feathers—ornaments
appropriate to spiritual and aristocratic beings—appear again in the poem as jewels gathered by the goddess herself. Her epiphany is accompanied by

The singing drum of Feng I,
The clear song of Nü Kua.

(Feng I was a water spirit, sometimes identified with
the God of the Yellow River.) There are also dragons,
clouds, whales, and waterfowl.[30] However, the goddess is forcibly established as an historical character,
fitted out with the factitious attributes of a deity and
the recognizable trappings of an empress. Ts'ao Chih's
poem apparently made a considerable impression, not
only on literary men but also on artists. Szu-ma Shao,
posthumously styled Ming Ti, ruled over the remnant
of the Chin nation for a brief period early in the fourth
century. He was reputed to be a skilled painter of Buddhist subjects and executed a "Picture of the Rhapsody
on the Divinity of the Lo."[31] The painting has not survived. The well-known painting of the Lo Goddess by
the famous Ku K'ai-chih, now extant in the form of a
later copy, was probably also intended as an illustra-
tion of the notorious euhemerizing poem.

## THE HAN WOMAN

The Han is one of China's notable rivers. Its name is
celebrated in many ways, most prominently as the title
of a great nation ruled over by the Liu dynasty at the
beginning of our era. That its deity would be a greatly

honored one is a reasonable expectation—but a false one. The worship of the spirit of the Han was, like that of the Ho, considered appropriate in the third century B.C. Doubtless it was worshipped at an earlier date as well. Early glosses suggest that it was a female spirit.[32] But later references to the "Woman of the Han" tend to be rather perfunctory and casual. Yang Hsiung refers to

> The Han woman submerged in the water;
> With bizarre beings, dark and obscure.

This is in a context of conventional peacocks, halcyons, and precious stones.[33] Later Tso Szu notices her briefly in a paean to the great city of Szechwan:

> The courtesan of Pa strums her strings,
> The woman of Han beats out the rhythm.[34]

The "Courtesan of Pa" appears to be a version of the Goddess of Shamanka Mountain, rightfully though peripherally in Szechwan. The Han Woman seems to have been courteously admitted to her company as an honorable tributary. But these divine musicians are little more than agreeable parts of the furniture, like St. Cecilia performing modestly at a grand court ball. Later still (we are now at the end of the fifth century), Chiang Yen, a literary patron both of glamour and of gramary, wrote more than once about the beauties of water goddesses. One unnamed nymph, styled merely "The Divine Woman over the Water," illuminates a poem which describes a mystic voyage in fantastic realms. It glows rhapsodically around her lovely but indistinct figure, discernible on the shore of a deep blue pool:

Beclouded and hazy she is—yet neither cloud nor fog:
Like most—like aurora,
All lights—all colors!

In short, she is a deity made manifest in rainbow
mist—a colorful but almost invisible fairy in the manner of Sung Yü's goddess.[35] Chiang has a few words to
tell about the Han Woman in another poem. There she
is a rather sad but unimportant figure in a setting
highly reminiscent of the *Ch'u tz'u,* full of magical
allusions to supernatural female beauty.[36] The little
goddess—for such she seems—fares no more signifi-
cantly in later literature. Lacking a considerable ode or
narrative composed by an eminent author entirely in
her honor, she has slid away into the closets and corners of literary history, an unnoticed waif and fading
ghost. We need not trouble to trace her pallid image in
T'ang literature.

Neither of the goddesses of the Lo and Han rivers
fared very well in early medieval cult. I have found no
trace of their shrines in T'ang texts. The Lo River itself, however, remained officially numinous. On June
6, 688, a "precious chart"—possibly modeled on
the "Lo Document" of antiquity—revealing a magic
square, was found in the river. Shortly thereafter this
treasure was awarded the name "Heaven-Given Hallowed Document," a title reflected in the adoption by
the Empress Wu of a new era name in 690: "Heaven
Given." The river itself was accordingly renamed
"Ever Glorious Lo Water," and its deity was honored
with the title "Illustrious and Hallowed Marklord."
Angling in its holy waters was forbidden.[37] There is no

trace here of the beloved goddess: her personality has been totally assimilated to the newly designated feudal lord.

## THE HSIANG CONSORT

Of all the classic water goddesses, the twinned lady of the Hsiang must have received most public honor in T'ang times, to judge from the relatively abundant information that still survives about her shrines. The primary haunt of the goddess, the nucleus of her cult, was in Lake Tung-t'ing. The lake's name, "Grotto Court," suggests that it was once regarded as a kind of courtyard or annex to the underground grottoes that were thought to permeate the whole land, linking together the subterranean realms of the Taoist immortals and other supernatural beings, who were there concealed and protected by the great mountains, themselves foci of celestial energy. Into this magic mere flowed many rivers, elements of a complex network of waters of every size and shape—a confluence known since antiquity as "the gateway of the Nine Rivers."[38] In Sung times, at least, it was said: "The divinities of the water attend the levee at Chün shan."[39] The image is that of a host of inflowing vassals paying formal allegiance to the paramount deity of the great lake, enthroned and holding court on its chief island.

The major river of the complex was the Hsiang, flowing northward through Hunan, carrying with it the waters of its important southern tributary, the Hsiao, to meet other lesser streams near its outlet. From the west and northwest came the Yüan and the

Li. The overflow from the lake poured into the vast Kiang where it passed nearby, coming from the sacred gorge of Wu shan and heading eastward toward the ocean. It was this vast domain and the region south of it that was ruled by the potent goddess, the daughter of Heaven.

The region was also associated with the name of Fan Li, a culture hero and possibly a real person, who strayed far from his traditional home in ancient Yüeh. Many natural features here bore his name, and it was said that he dwelt in the midst of the lake, transformed from a semi-legendary philosopher of nature and adviser of kings into a kind of water deity.[40]

The cult center of this vast playground for water spirits and connoisseurs of water was on the mainland in a region on the east shore of the lake that came to be known as Pa-ling. Its official name in T'ang times was sometimes Yüeh-yang and sometimes Yüeh-chou. This is where the waters of the lake merged with those of the Hsiang and the Kiang—but then their shores were certainly contoured differently than now. This worshipful place was at the northern limit of the goddess's domain; still it remained the most ancient and venerable heart of that domain. It had been a sacred center in the distant past, belonging to the marshes of Yün-meng "Cloud Dream," extending north and south on both sides of the Kiang,[41] in the kingdom of Ch'u:

> To the north it communicates with Shamanka Gorge;
> To the south it reaches its limit with Hsiao and Hsiang.[42]

Another way of putting it was "Pa-ling is the vortex of Hsiao and Hsiang."[43] This means that the lake and its ancient shrine were the receptacle and abyss of the long rivers that drained the lands to the south. Here too, near the north shore of the lake, was the "North Holm" *(pei chu),* a place sacred to the goddess in her guise as "God's Child" since the days when the "Nine Songs" were fresh and new.[44]

The name Pa-ling was, in medieval tradition, reminiscent of primordial serpents—and hence of dragons. Pa-ling means "Tumulus of Pa," suggesting a royal barrow, the repository of sacred remains. Pa is a rather mysterious word. Geographically it is associated with the nearer part of Szechwan, and philologically with a mythical snake. Medieval tradition had it that the name referred to a pile of gigantic bones, left by the rotting corpse of a monstrous elephant-eating serpent that had been butchered by the primordial archer I.[45]

Already in antiquity Pa-ling was known as a prosperous and bountiful region. "The Canon of Mountains and Seas" told that this land was rich in gold and silver ores and abounded in tangerines, pomeloes, herbaceous peonies, thorn apples, and mistflowers. The goddess—or goddesses, as this text has it—enjoyed these verdant surroundings, which she herself kept fertile. She appeared there in "whirling winds and violent rain."[46] In Han times the region was populated by simple hunters, fishers, and rice farmers who practiced fire-field and hoe cultivation. They were noted, like most southerners, for their devotion to shamanistic arts and to unauthorized religious rites.[47] Later, the T'ang history notes the availability of soft-shell turtles, ramie fabrics, and a profitable iron deposit.[48] The region was also known for its fine tea and for a gourmet specialty—caviar. The natives made an excellent variety of this delicacy, of which they were inordinately fond. They simmered the roes of the Yangtze sturgeon in a decoction of the seeds of a kind of honey locust *(Gleditschia sinensis).* Salt was added, and the eggs allowed to steep in the solution.[49]

The domain of the goddess was vast and fruitful, but as her worship tended to be concentrated around Lake Tung-t'ing, she had perforce to share these rich and sacred shores with other divine creatures, many of them showing themselves in female guise just like herself. Some of these beings appear anonymously and briefly in gazetteers. An example is the tale of a woodcutter on White Crane Mountain at Pa-ling. His story is included in an official description of the township compiled at the beginning of the Sung dynasty.[50] The man met a supernatural being at the Platform of the Purple Cercis (that is, redbud) and was given an iron flute which played soundless music. He blew it one day and two women appeared, to the sound of thunder. They presented him with an herb of immortality, and promised him eternal life beneath the waves. The account concludes laconically: "presumably they were dragon women." It is easy to see in them also the figures of the Consorts of the Hsiang.

No particular shrine is identifiable in this case, but the gazetteers note the existence of such structures, even when they do not identify the deity worshipped in them. Here is an example from the tenth century: "The West Lake Temple is located west of the township; a water deity is worshipped there."[51] Sometimes the deity is not only anonymous but also quite ambiguous—she looks at us from many faces. Such is the spirit evoked in Li Ho's poem entitled "Temple of the Divine Woman of Lotus Fragrance." This is an evocation of an unknown mountain and river goddess, with associations with the poet's home in Honan. She swims in a medley of misty epithets, once the property of other goddesses.[52] The composite nymph, because she meets the God of the Kiang rather than the King of Ch'u, has some of the attributes of the Wu shan goddess, but as the same time she is an obvious avatar of the Hsiang Lady. The Goddess of the Lo also participates in her characterization. She is *the* goddess of the waters of central China.[53]

A number of poems record impressions of a temple of the goddess without specifying its locality, although it is presumably on the shores of the great lake. This shrine is commonly styled "Temple of the Hsiang Consort[s]" and could refer either to the "Yellow Tumulus" temple on the mainland, which we shall inspect presently, to the temple on the island nearby, or possibly to some other shrine of the goddess. Typical is a sequence of trivial poems preserved in the "Complete T'ang Poetry," collectively titled "Temple of the Hsiang Consort" *(Hsiang fei miao).*[54] They are said to have been written by human guests who were entertained by the goddess in the privacy of her sanctum. One, for instance, is entitled "Composed by [Ts'ui] Wo in Appreciation of a Meeting with the Consort of the Hsiang on Her Own Mat." It is unexciting quatrain, full of sweet allusions to birds in springtime, divine palaces, dancing phoenixes, all climaxed by a soulful "I thought I must be in a dream, at Yangt'ai"—pleasant eroticism, blending all experiences with goddesses into the ultimate vision of the Divine

Woman at Yang-t'ai in ancient Ch'u. There are better poems on the goddess's shrine.

Tu Fu's ode on the Temple of Consort goes like this:[55]

> Stately and solemn—the Temple of the Hsiang Consort.
> Spring, and dark blue water by vacant walls.
> Insects trace characters in the moss on her jade girdle.
> Swallows dance in the dust on her halcyon canopy.
>
> I moor at evening, ascend through the trees of
>     the mud flat.
> For its slight aroma I borrow pepperwort from the isle.
> Her grief at Ts'ang-wu was not shallow:
> Staining tears lie on thick bamboo clumps.

(The shrine appears to be untended. The image of the goddess is in poor repair; insects scrawl trails through her moss-covered apparel, and birds raise the dust from the temple furniture. The "isle" can hardly be the rocky mount out in the lake where there was a major sanctuary of the goddess: the Chinese word connotes a small sandbank or similar undistinguished eyot. The poet needs a fragrant offering for the goddess—and finds handy only the moss we call pepperwort. Conclusion: appropriately classical emotions about the death of Shun.)

Tu Fu's contemporary Liu Ch'ang-ch'ing wrote a double quatrain of somewhat similar character, although the Wu shan goddess and the forlorn King of Ch'u are more prominent in it than is Shun. The temple is deserted among ancient trees. A desolate expanse of water foams nearby. Lichen has formed on the goddess's beaded shoes; weeds grow on her gauzy blouse.[56] As elsewhere, the body and costume of the goddess are easily assimilated to the natural surroundings.

Poems of Li Ch'ün-yü and Kao P'ien[57] written in the ninth century, both titled "Temple of the Hsiang Consort," add a few more details, such as the painted furnishings inside the shrine and the spotted bamboo outside it, but we learn little else that will help us to visualize the temple as the site of actual religious practices. One suspects that it was a popular place among educated men, and was doubtless kept in reasonably good condition by responsible officials, if only to maintain the good name of their district among visiting, possibly influential notables from the capital.

The "Temple of the Yellow Tumulus" *(huang ling miao)* stood in Hsiang-yin *hsien* in Yüeh-chou, where the Hsiang River debouched into the great lake.[58] In some form or other it had stood there for a very long time. The *Shui ching chu* takes note of a "temple to the two consorts" at this spot, adding that "in our times we call it 'Temple of the Yellow Tumulus.'"[59] The bohemian genius Li Ch'ün-yü visited it early in the ninth century, and composed a poem to celebrate the event. The reverend but beautiful goddesses stood in a rustic edifice overlooking the river. There was an ancient stele whose inscription was obliterated. Everything was covered with weeds. The sun sets; the cuckoo sobs sadly; the goddesses are eternally separated from their ancient mate.[60] It is a good poem, but no cliché, however well rephrased, is overlooked.

A familiar spirit of this region, Li Ch'ün-yü, also wrote a poem for a friend at a pavilion by the river at Hsiang-yin. In it he refers to the "Shrine of God's Child" *(Ti tzu tz'u)*. The name can only refer to the

Lady of the Hsiang, and the place is presumably the Yellow Tumulus Temple. This is not a reverent poem. The setting is merely an occasion for revery and communal pensiveness: the sky is deep blue, the spring flowers flood the estuary with perfume, the troublesome past is like a fading dream.[61]

Fortunately, in 819, when Han Yü was on his way to exile in Ch'ao-chou, he stopped at this shrine. Fearing for his health and even for his life in the malarial tropics, he offered prayers seeking the protection of the goddesses. Through divination they gave him a favorable sign. In 820 he was recalled to the court and, almost overcome with gratitude, he composed a "sacrificial address" to them. Despite his objections to Buddhism, the famous writer was cautious and attentive—almost devout—in the carrying out of properly sanctioned attentions to orthodox deities. Perusal of the texts of his sacrificial address to the fearful crocodiles of Ch'ao-chou and of his account of the restoration of services due to the God of the South Sea should persuade any possibly skeptical reader. In his new religious text, he vows to restore the dilapidated temple where "cattle and goats enter the building, but neither the folk who dwell here nor travelling merchants come to make sacrifice and offerings." (This adds some support to my suspicion that the deserted fane of the goddesses described by earlier visitors was in fact this "Temple of the Yellow Tumulus.") Han Yü promised to have the building brightly painted and offered a personal gift of 100,000 cash in support of the restoration. He also vowed to reerect an old stele, doubtless the same one mentioned in Li Ch'ün-yü's poem, whose text had been obliterated by the elements. In its place he proposed to compose a new one, "in order greatly to stimulate the manifestation of the awesome divinity of the Mistress and the Lady."[62] The text of the inscription that he had engraved on the old tablet, which was re-erected in 821, has come down to us. It begins:

> On the edge of the Hsiang there is a temple called "Yellow Tumulus." It has stood there from some earlier age for the worship of the two daughters of Yao, who were the two consorts of Shun. In the courtyard there was a stone stele, broken and rent apart, its fragments scattered over the ground. The text was broken up and defective. I looked into the "Illustrated Record" and it said ... that a stele had been erected in Han times, inscribed "Lady of the Hsiang."[63]

Han Yü goes on to say that he inspected the fragments himself and found that the ruined stele was not the Han one. It had actually been erected in A.D. 288, and was inscribed "The Two Consorts of the Divine King of Yü"—that is, of Shun. He appends a discussion of the different names and titles given to the goddesses. It presents the standard view for T'ang times, except that it rejects the tradition that Shun died and was buried in Ts'ang-wu and that the two consorts tried in vain to find him and finally were drowned. He prefers a religious rather than a euhemerizing, historical interpretation of the legends: Shun and the two consorts did not die but became great divinities. They are worthy of sacrifice by the people, and indeed all persons traversing this river should give them due honor. In conclusion he recounts the story of his grateful pledge to restore the temple.

The other sacred site in Lake Tung-t'ing was Chün shan, or Tung-t'ing shan, the considerable island in the lake west of Pa-ling township.[64] Unfortunately the lower parts of the island were frequently flooded, especially during the summer and autumn months, making it very difficult of access to visitors.[65] The name of the island, depending on the preference of the commentator, might refer to the "Mistress of the Hsiang" or to some other sovereign, real or mythical. The island was also called "Grotto Court Mountain," that is, the mountain in Grotto Court Lake. The rocky island concealed a mystic palace with five gateways that led by strange and hidden passages to numinous mountains, among them O-mei in Szechwan, Lo-fou in Kwangtung, and T'ai-shan in Shantung—all of them seats of divine potentates highly regarded in early medieval times. Some men said that the island had not always been in the lake. The ninth-century poet Fang Kan, a superficially uncouth fellow—a gem in the rough—reported that,

> In the beginning it was a rock on the summit
>     of Mount K'un-lun,
> Blown by a sea wind, it fell into Lake Tung-t'ing.[66]

A strange sea wind indeed, blowing out of the holy highlands of Central Asia. But possibly Fan Kan invented this rumor himself, to give honor to the divine island. The divine wave-lapped island was also, it was said, dignified by the presence of a great sovereign long ago: Liu Ch'e, better known as Wu Ti of Han, climbed its side and shot a kraken to death there.[67] Doubtless this act demonstrated the heroism of the monarch, but it seems an unwarranted deed of violence against a courtier of the great goddess.

The island had been famed from early times for its sourpeel tangerines, and a tenth-century monastery had a fine orchard of them.[68] In the same period there was a spring of sweet wine there. To drink from it made one immortal. But, although the monks could often smell pleasant whiffs of it in the springtime, they could never find it.[69] Fortunately we have an account of the island's "Temple of the Mistress of the Hsiang" written in the second half of the ninth century by Li Mi-szu, who was at that time chief magistrate of the township of Pa-ling.[70] It begins like this:

> Grotto Court Mountain is surely one of the grotto-archives of the divine transcendents. It is because of that courtyard of a grotto archive that the lake has been called by this name, and since high antiquity the same has been true of the mountain. Some man of old erected a shrine to the Lady of the Hsiang on this mountain, so that it is also called "The Lady's Mountain." Under the Illustrious One of Ch'in the temple and its precincts were destroyed by burning, and for long after that there was no one to roof or thatch it. This mountain is twenty *li* from the outer wall of the county seat, but people nearby have never ventured to dwell on it. According to the "Illustrated Canon" this mountain will not admit filth or evil, and it lacks wild beasts. My humble view: in the sea there are the likes of Round Peak *(Yüan Chiao)* and P'eng Seamount *(P'eng Tao)*, which, although visible from afar, may not be reached by men. But *this* mountain, a mere anthill or swelling in the heart of the waves, encircled on all sides by clouds and water, can be reached by men—but they cannot dwell there. Surely it is not inferior to Round Peak and

P'eng Seamount? Indeed it is right that it should be relied on and trusted by divine and numinous beings!

Our author continues to tell how sacrifices used to be made here when there were droughts or floods, but adds that it was a long time since these could be properly performed because of the dilapidated condition of the fane. There was a drought at Pa-ling in the summer of 861, during his incumbency as governor. Accordingly he purified himself and took a boat to the island, against the advice of his subordinates who said that the passage was dangerous. He had himself rowed over anyhow. There he offered his prayers at the foot of the mountain under the blazing sun. Clouds arose. The wind shifted. The boat returned easily, to general rejoicing. When he reached his office the rain began to fall. "Then I knew," he wrote, "that unless it had been a supreme divinity it would not have been able to move both *yin* and *yang*." He decided to erect a place of worship on the island, but the press of business prevented the achievement of this project until two years later. Indeed, he boasted that the region under his jurisdiction remained free from disasters, and that rainfall was always appropriate to the season after the building of the temple (text written 7 June 863).

Always, if they were diligent in the performance of their duties, Chinese magistrates in the provinces served as priests of the official religion. In this case the goddess was afforded more than perfunctory status because of the gratitude of the magistrate, even though continuous adoration of her was pretty much ruled out because of the remoteness of her temple out in the midst of the wind-tossed waters.

Although the whole drainage system of the Hsiang River and its tributaries was the domain of the goddess, her worship was chiefly concentrated around Lake Tung-t'ing. But there was a lesser focus of worship around the headwaters of the Hsiang River—a region famed for the numinous presence of her supposed husband Shun. Roughly this second area corresponded to the Ling-ling district (also called, in T'ang times, Yung-chou) and the region south of there, through the source of the Hsiang, and over the watershed to the headwaters of the Kuei River in northern Kwangsi.[71]

It is said that in the earliest times the hero Shun undertook a patrol of the distant and barbarous southland, that he died in Ts'ang-wu, and that he was buried on the Mountain of Nine Uncertainties *(Chiu i shan)*.[72] Wherever this region may have been thought to be in very early times, in the historic period it has been located in southernmost Hunan, on the Kwangsi border, a rugged forested zone lying close to the Tropic of Cancer. The fork of the two upper branches of the Hsiang River takes form just north of here. Here also rises the Li River, joined to the Hsiang system in T'ang times by a high-level canal; it flows southward to connect with larger streams and ultimately to yield its waters to the South China Sea at Canton. The western branch of the fork of the Hsiang, which rejoices in the same name as the great river itself, rises not far from Kuei-lin and passes by Ling-ling. The eastern branch is called the Hsiao and rises near Lien-chou in northern Kwangtung. It meets its sister stream at Ling-ling. These headwaters are sacred to Shun, and by extension to his two consorts. Moreover, because the latter came to be identified with the Hsiang goddess, that lady's domain was therefore extended this far south. But there she was overshadowed by the towering figure of the male hero.[73] Some say that after his death and burial, the consorts too died and were buried on Mount Heng, the sacred mountain of the south. Others deny this.[74] In any case, Shun retained the mysterious Mount of the Nine Uncertainties to himself. The story of his interment there is very ancient,[75] and that event along with the tale of his wives is perpetuated in the names that were given to the nine bewildering peaks by T'ang times, if not earlier. By then Shun had long since been transformed from a primordial deity with a strong hint of the elephantine about him into a respectably human-visaged sage-king stereotype. A few of these names are "Peak of Fairy Radiance," "Peak of Shun's Spring," and "Peak of Maiden Bloom." The holy tomb itself was reputed to have been beneath the Peak of Maiden Bloom.[76] An ancillary legend holds that the body of Shun was lost, and that two heavenly ladies shed copious tears as they searched along the Hsiang River for it. Their tears stained the surface of the bamboos that grew there in abundance, and this explains the origins of the famous spotted bamboos *(Phyllostachys puberula* var. *boryana)* of south China,[77] much admired for making fine walking sticks, brush handles, and the like. The story of the tear spots became a cliché that no medieval poet could resist. It was sufficient only to make casual reference to this variety of bamboo to evoke automatic sentiments about the death of Shun and the doleful weeping of his wives.

The southernmost shrines of the goddess are veiled

in an obscurity that suggests neglect: "Grey-green, the temple of Yao's daughters."[78] The temple of the twinned goddess at the head of the Yüan River, described in the eighth century in this verse, was evidently covered with moss. But the shivering Shun gibbon—the same as the gibbon that howls with the voice of the King of Ch'u—is there, and so is a red leopard. The poet was Li Ch'i, seeing a friend off to those remote lands, and it was necessary to give due attention to such tropical wonders in a farewell poem in honor of a south-bound friend. A shrine at the headwaters of the Hsiang is better documented. When Liu Tsung-yüan, the superb essayist, was in Yung-chou, in a disgraceful exile from which he never returned, the Temple of the Two Consorts at the Source of the Hsiang was destroyed by fire. This was in the late August of 814. There was great consternation among the local authorities, who began a great effort at rebuilding. The restoration was completed and the temple rededicated on December 22 of the same year. A stele was erected at the gate, and the distinguished exile contributed a text to be inscribed on it. The language of this panegyric casts the goddesses in the roles of pious daughters and wives. It was written in formal, archaizing four-syllable verses, stylistically very unlike Liu Tsung-yüan's loosely constructed "records" *(chi)*.[79] This probably suited the town elders very well.

Later in the ninth century, on a visit to the former dwelling of a "delightful [that is, female] person" in Kuei-chou, Li Ch'ün-yü took the opportunity to compose a rather conventional quatrain in which he identified an absent sweetheart with the Hsiang goddess:

Kuei Water is as green as ever —
But the delightful person will never return.
She can only follow the evening rain,
Flying into the Hills of Nine Doubts.[80]

This offhand compliment to the fidelity of the goddess, and perhaps to that of her modern reincarnation, can hardly be taken as evidence of the actual survival of her cult here. Indeed we may not even assume that the poet visited her temple, if such existed.

Almost a century later, Chang Mi, in the service of the secessionist (or independent) state of (Southern) T'ang situated in a ruined fragment of the great T'ang empire in the ancient Wu area, stopped one evening at the source of the Hsiang. He immortalized in verse the soft sound of the waves lapping against his boat, the trees seen through the opaque drizzle, and the howling of leopards (not the usual gibbons!) through the mist. The trees on the bleak grounds of the temple of the two goddesses had grown old, he wrote, as had the memory of the goddesses and the hero they once mourned.[81] Was this the temple restored by Liu Tsung-yüan? Could it have been the shrine whose ruins were still pointed out to tourists of the southern Sung period, under the name of "Temple of the Hsiang Wife"?[82] We cannot be sure. In any event this was not a great cult center of the goddess. The shadow of Shun loomed too large. Nonetheless, note may also be taken of two shrines to the goddess not far away in Hunan, one in Tao-chou, one in Li-chou. These are remembered because of the notices of their survival as "ancient relics" in the Sung period, and it may be that they existed in T'ang times.[83]

# 3 The Great Water Goddesses in T'ang Poetry

Her playful Sea horse woos her soft commands,
Turns his quick ears, his webbed claws expands,
His watery way with waving volutes wins,
Or listening librates on unmoving fins.
The nymph emerging mounts her scaly seat,
Hangs o'er his glossy sides her silver feet.

*Erasmus Darwin*
"The Economy of Vegetation"

We have from the sixth century a poem by Liu Ling-hsien, one of three talented sisters of the Liang dynasty. In it she pictures herself as a beautiful woman answering a poem addressed to her by her husband. She examines herself in a mirror, looking for assurance that her beauty is comparable to lovely supernatural persons:

The moon at night suggests the Divine Woman;
The pink clouds of dawn image the Lo Consort.[1]

The Divine Woman must be the goddess of Wu shan, although the rosy clouds of morning are more appropriate to her than to the goddess of the Lo. Madame Liu has created an inexact pastiche which mingles the images of a number of goddesses. But in the end it is not the misty, radiant nymphs but herself that she celebrates. The secularization of the goddesses in literature was already well under way. This change is best revealed in the persona of the Lo goddess, who has few traceable classical antecedents, although the chain of her literary life is almost continuous after her vivid realization by Ts'ao Chih.

The old goddesses appear in the literature of T'ang times in various guises, but each has her own congenial habitat among the word constructions of T'ang writers. Nü Kua, for instance, fares best in folktales done in the literary language. She is inhuman, weird and scary, scaled or fishlike, close to rustic belief and cult. In contrast, the goddess of the Lo River is very like a pert, contemporary belle, almost a courtesan, and appears to best advantage in this guise in elegant prose fiction. She and some dragon kings' daughters visualized in this genre resemble the court belles of Europe imagined in polished literature as Greek nymphs and naiads. Lyric verse reveals the Lo Divinity in rather similar terms: she is everywhere a metaphor for a secular charmer, although for a few poets she remains a gossamer, moonlit sylph.

But T'ang poetry has another vision of the goddesses, almost completely restricted to that medium, and best exemplified in realizations of the Wu shan goddess. The typical mood is nostalgic—the conjuring up of an archaic, lovely, ghostly, unattainable being. This somewhat softened version of the rain woman apparently derives gradually, without sudden transformations, from the divine woman of Sung Yü. The Hsiang goddess stands somewhere between the Lo Divinity and the Divine Woman. She is less completely a pampered palace beauty, but also not entirely a shimmering spirit.

Before looking at these goddesses in T'ang poetry, let us take note of a T'ang poem written *by* a goddess. A certain Ho Kuang-yüan enjoyed the temporary love—it was always so—of a dragon woman. He addressed three poems to her, and she wrote a quatrain in reply to each of his. Because poems composed by supernatural beings are comparatively rare, it has seemed worthwhile to translate an example into English. Here, then, is one of the stanzas written by "The Dragon Woman of Luminous Moon Pool."² Doubtless concealing her scales, she holds out the prospect of a romantic interlude:

> I sit long, the wind blows, the green damask is cold.
> Through the nine heavens the moon shines,
>     a plate of crystal water.
> Do not think "She will turn back, plunge, sink, be gone!"
> For you, regrets in this springtime light—
>     and just one night of joy.

(The green damask is metaphorical for the shining green surface of her pool; the nine heavens are the nine parts of the sky—eight directions plus center; the Chinese regarded rock crystal as petrified water.) The fortunate Mr. Ho replies with a soulful quatrain suggesting that a single night of love would reconcile him to an eternity of separation.

NÜ KUA

T'ang poets paid little attention to the most venerable dragon of them all, Nü Kua. She had become a legend for mythographers, and an embarrassingly feminine monarch of a golden age for conventional historians. Still, her name turns up occasionally. It is pleasant to find that Li Po remembered her as the creatrix of mankind:

> Nü Kua played with the yellow earth,
> Patted it into ignorant, inferior Man.[3]

She even retained something of her dignity in the unusual guise of a vast, earth-shadowing deity, coterminous with the blue sky, in a fragment of a lost poem by Ch'in T'ao-yü, who wrote at the end of the ninth century:

> Nü Kua's gauzy skirt, a hundred feet long,
> Suspended over the Hsiang and Kiang, gives its
>    color to the hills.[4]

Even without a context, we can see the flowing skirt of the goddess who repaired the sky, drifting from horizon to horizon (the "hundred feet" is typical of Chinese estimates of celestial distances), shedding its blue on the dark hills of the great rivers of the south, and we are reminded of verses about the temple at Shamanka Mountain which also revealed parts of its goddess's countenance dispersed across the landscape.

THE DIVINE WOMAN

Poems—that is, lyrics in the *shih* form—about the rainbow goddess of Sung Yü's dramatic rhapsodies are abundant in post-Han times. Many of them reflect the manner and matter of the Han *yüeh fu* titled "Shaman Mountain is High!" *(Wu shan kao)*. These are not uncommon during the interval of invasion and divison between Han and T'ang, but it appears, from a rough survey of extant collections, that the type is most common of all in the T'ang period. They do not all show the same form and structure by any means, but are united by their common theme. But again, they do not treat that theme always in the same way. Some poems are simple, some are complex; some are plain, some are fantastic. Most make polite nods toward the shadow of Sung Yü, either by way of easy allusions to his work, or—very commonly—by lifting phrases directly from it. "Dawn clouds" and "evening rain," the harbingers or disguises of the goddess, are only the most common of many. A typical verse is:

> Dawn clouds and evening rain—linked through
> the dark of the sky.[5]

Such is the path and promise of the goddess in hundreds of stanzas. But, as we shall see, these meteoric glimpses, however much akin in theme, do not mean the same thing to different poets. Possibly the most consistent scent that perfuses poems about the goddess is sexuality, whether overt or subtly disguised.

The motif of physical love between a living person and a ghost appears everywhere in Chinese folklore and literature. It is particularly prominent in the always popular tales of fantasy. Probably it is best exemplified in the T'ang *ch'uan ch'i*. There it typically takes the form of the love affair of a fox fairy and a handsome youth. Revitalized and strengthened by his youthful ardor, the ghostly beauty can assume palpable physical attributes, and perhaps even return to the land of the living.[6]

Not only can the soul of a man on a distant journey visit his wife in a dream and make her pregnant, but his spirit can effectively cohabit with her after his physical death. This is the inner and ultimate meaning of the Wu shan fable. The king's affair with the goddess takes place in a "dream," that is, in a supernatural world. It adds an element of divine sanction to his rule, and so brings prosperity to his land and people. At the same time, the divine woman is rejuvenated and realized more solidly and vibrantly. In exchange for the gift of fertilizing power, she gains life.

This idea turns up in all kinds of obscure corners of Chinese culture. An excellent example from T'ang poetry is Li Ho's strange setting of the *Wu shan kao* theme—a theme he would hardly have neglected.[7] At first glance an almost impenetrable tangle of images and compacted allusions, his poem seems to defy translation into English. The syllabic count is 3/3/7/7/7/7/7/7/7. Despite its lushness and the familiar Li Ho magic, it remains a scholar's poem. An English version must be hazarded, but a commentary is unavoidable.

Indigo—dense woods,
High, piercing heaven.
By great Kiang's flopping surges: a deity with
    trails of mist;
A soul from Ch'u pursuing a dream: a wind
    of typhoon force.
Daybreak fogs and flying rain breed coins of lichen.

Turquoise Courtesan: once gone, it's for
    a thousand years.
In lilac scent and cane bamboos she makes that
    old gibbon howl.
Her ancient shrine, so near the moon—cold with toad
    and cinnamon.
But fagara droops its red in the crevice of
    a moist cloud.

This may be rudely explicated as follows:

The mountain slopes are covered with gloomy woods.

The mountain seems to disappear in the sky.

The river churns wildly through the gorge; near it, also a
    wild vision, is a spirit trailing evanescent mists like a
    gown.

The ghost of Hsiang Wang of Ch'u tries to recapture the
    goddess of his faded dream: he appears as a tempes-
    tuous blast.

The endless precipitation covers the boulders and cliffs
    with lichens (commonly called "lichen coins," from
    their shape; there seems to be a lost trope here.)

But the goddess herself comes only once in a thousand
    years.

Her presence arouses the lust (as her absence the anguish)
    of an ape, who represents the king.

Her temple, silhouetted against the moon, is infected with
    the cold of the frozen toad and cinnamon tree that
    live on that satellite.

A pink fagara flower (*Zanthoxylum simulans,* used as a
    pungent condiment like pepper) dips into a breach in
    a cloud—which is in fact the goddess. A millennial
    copulation is at last achieved. (For fagara as a male
    sex symbol, see *Shih ching* "T'ang feng," Chiao liao.)

Similar images survive in the songs of the folk of south China and southeast Asia. For instance, among the songs of the modern "boat people" of Hong Kong are many which show parallels to elements in the *Ch'u tz'u*. Among these are sexual images in the form of botanical allusions. These remind us in many ways of the floral tropes employed by such medieval poets as Li Ho. In one wedding song discovered among these "simple" folk, the bride is an orange tree; she is fertilized by rain; she bears fruit and is happy. In another she is plainly presented as the divine woman of Shamanka Mountain expecting the spirit of her husband, the fecundating king.[8] Such folk survivals as these are at once more frank and more conservative than the lyrics of most T'ang literati. But surely these same medieval writers, who used the ancient classical language, drew on living traditions like those of modern Hong Kong, as much as on stylish literary prototypes. Liu Yü-hsi, for instance, tried to reshape the shamanistic songs of the old Ch'u region in conformity with the classical *Ch'u tz'u* styles that had their origin in the same area in early antiquity.[9] Such evidence of attention to the vernacular is not common, but it is compelling.

Imagery—fagara and orange—is not the whole of poetry, but it is a most significant part of it. It is highly significant in the Wu shan poems. Convention demands it. George Santayana said with reason: "Conventions do not arise without some reason, and genius will know how to rise above them by a fresh appreciation of their rightness, and will feel no temptation to overturn them in favour of personal whimsies."[10] A good poet will know how to appreciate and revivify a great image, however often mediocre poets may have debased it. Great subjects can inspire mediocre poems, while apt metaphors can be downgraded by second-class poets. The fagara makes Li Ho's poem continuous with the great poetic tradition, but the way he exploits the image is entirely novel.

The motif of spiritual and physical regeneration through the agency of a divine sexual experience, classically demonstrated in the Wu shan poems, demands the traditional framework and the traditional embroidery. These may even be employed for adverse effect. To the late ninth-century poet Su Cheng, the sexuality of clouds and rain was merely an aberration. He suggested that the myth of the shaman woman was a base superstition, leading to lewdness:

> In former times too were clouds and rain—
> In present times as well are clouds and rain.
> Hence when wild depravity abounds
> Men meet in dreams the woman of Shaman Mountain.

> Up to now even a paragon—an enlightened monarch—
> Might heed such weird goblin talk;
> But nowadays the clouds above those peaks
> Yield freely only freedom from care.[11]

This clear, purged, and exorcized landscape has its attractions, but most T'ang poets did not seem to care for it. As to the "enlightened monarch," it is probable that the poet was expressing his enthusiasm for his own sovereign's freedom from superstition. Possibly he is referring to the unfortunate Chao Tsung, or possibly to the first Liang emperor.

If, ignoring differences in tone and attitude, we sur-

vey the whole vast array of standard images in the
Wu shan poems of T'ang times, they seem monotonous: endless reiterations of rain-soaked mountainsides,
swirling mists, blinding cloudbanks, howling gibbons,
and shrieking winds. But of course we must not treat
every wisp of cloud and every drop of rain in a Wu
shan poem as if it were just like its namesakes in a hundred other poems. Li Ho's gibbon and Li Ho's rain, for
instance, are certainly not typical of the genera. But before going on to look at some fine instances of novel
exploitation of familiar images, let us inspect a few less
original usages—they are not necessarily bad ones.

The creation of illusions and phantasms—such as
deceptive appearances of the fragmented goddess and
the ghostly king as elements of the landscape—has already been anticipated in the brief discussion of the
development of the Nü Kua legend. This love of hallu-
cinations is common in the ruck of Wu shan poems.
But some of them go beyond the hallucinatory to the
incredibly identical: the goddess becomes an actual
part of the natural world. Often it is hard to tell where
it is identity or only similitude that is intended. Is the
"divine woman cloud"[12] the cloud that accompanies
the divine woman, or the cloud that is the divine woman? Is the "divine woman rain"[13] the goddess's rain or
the goddess who is rain? There is no way to tell. Is
"manner of rain, demeanor of cloud"[14] to be regarded
as a simile of the goddess's movements, as a symbol of
her secret nature, or as an affirmation of her true being? Only occasionally is a simile quite explicit, as in
"Shrouded crag, like ghost or spirit!"[15] It is probable
that many writers, at least, were keenly aware that na-

ture was animated by divine beings—that rivers, clouds, and crags were the physical manifestations of the supernatural world. The fact is apparent in the whole hierarchy of the officially recognized high gods of T'ang: the most exalted were the stars, plainly so designated—no need to write "star spirits." The things themselves were numinous. So also the seas and hills were living entities, unique in their dignity. The poets of T'ang accepted this without question.

Still, irrespective of their divinity or possibly because of it, the splendors of nature were worth pondering for their own sake. If Wu shan was a haunted mountain, it was also a very picturesque mountain. The literary pilgrims who visited the celebrated site, whatever thrills they may have felt at the immanence of an archaic deity, were often moved by the prospect of spray-spattered rocks and mist-hidden woodlands. Some of their poems show a correspondingly greater attention to the natural splendors and aerial displays of the region. An example is a poem of Shen Ch'üanch'i,[16] which begins and ends conventionally enough, but contains two unusual lines:

Lightning [-cast] shadows fall before the Kiang;
Thunder [-made] sounds lengthen beyond the gorge.

This is a considerable improvement on the usual clouds, mists, winds, and rain. On the other hand, an effusion primarily concerned with the weather could sometimes lead the reader to the goddess rather than away from her. Li Chiao, an early T'ang poet, wrote a series of stanzas on meteorological, physiographic, and other natural phenomena, descending even to ap-

ricots and magpies. One of them, entitled simply
"Rain,"[17] begins with a fine anthropomorphizing effect:

> Northwest—a skin of cloud arises!
> Southeast—feet of rain approach!

It comes as no surprise, then, when the Divine Woman
appears two verses later—an animating presence behind these striding nimbus limbs.

A final word on the evolution of the Wu shan theme
in late T'ang times. The gifted Li Hsün celebrated the
exotic pleasures and hazards of the tropical south in a
brilliant series of *tz'u* set to the tune *Nan hsiang tzu*.
Probably he was the first to add a certain nonclassical
or barbaric glamour to the genre.[18] He also composed
a pair of *tz'u* in the mode *Wu shan i tuan yün* "One
Strip of Cloud at Shamanka Mountain."[19] The syllabic form is 5/5/7/5/ /5/5/7/5. The two poems are related in meaning, the first leading into the second. A
stranger appears, rowing his boat to shore in Shamanka Gorge. He meditates on the old story as he sadly
contemplates the empty, rain-drenched shrine. The
second section goes something like this:

> The ancient temple leans against a blue-green barrier;
> A mobile palace is pillowed on the cyan flow.
> Water sound and mountain color lock up her
>     high boudoir—
> Such bygone things are dim and distant in the mind.
>
> Clouds and rain—dawn and evening too.
> Mist and flowers—spring as well as autumn.
> A shrieking gibbon: why must it approach a lonely boat?
> The wayfaring stranger has brought too much
>     gloom on himself!

Commentary:

> The goddess's shrine is backed by the dark forest.
> The "mobile palace" is presumably the visitor's boat.
> Her inner sanctum is enclosed by her own natural
>      attributes.
> The truth about her nature is impenetrable.
>
> The atmospherics are perpetual.
> (Again.)
> The cry of the ape, identified with the ancient king,
>      is superfluous:
> The poet's mood was despondent enough
>      without that too.

This is a handsome treatment of an often treated subject, but it lacks the innovating spirit of Li Hsün's *Nan hsiang tzu* poems.

Some poets, endowed with a special talent for the unusual and even the bizarre, made poems about the goddess that show much more originality than the conventional exercises of their contemporaries. My examples are, not surprisingly, selected from the writings of three madmen, Li Po, Meng Chiao, and Li Ho.

Li Po was especially addicted to the subject, apparently infatuated wth its capacity for yielding supernatural atmospheres. It is possible that he wrote more lyrics on the theme of Shamanka Mountain and its familiar spirit than any other T'ang poet.[20] In the example which follows, he introduces the name of Sung Yü himself. Suddenly we are not transforming a myth, but attempting to estimate the intention of the mythographer.[21]

> Turquoise Courtesan, daughter of heaven's god:
> Prismatic soul transformed to clouds of dawn,

Coiled gently into dreamy nighttime,
No heart to face the Lord of Ch'u.

A brocade coverlet blankets the autumn moon,
A damask matting voids the orchid scent.
Dim and dark: who can plumb it to the end?
An insubstantial tale—the text of Sung Yü.

Normal at first, though strangely phrased, the poem concludes with a couplet that departs radically from the tradition. Is it simply a skeptical view? Is it disillusionment? Does it say something about the futility of human love? I am not ready to say. Li Po, as often, is baffling.

Somewhat similar to this is a poem by a little known ninth-century writer named Yü Fen. It is even more strongly reminiscent of the puritanical effusion of Su Cheng, translated earlier. Yü Fen is remembered chiefly for his resistance to the rage for tone-patterned, embellished poetry that characterized his age. His rhetorical (and unpopular) repetitions and ingenious rhymes make the analogy with Li Po's work particularly interesting.[22]

What hill lacks clouds at dawn?
These clouds too are bleak and faded.
What hill lacks evening rain?
This rain too is a gray expanse.
Sung Yü, confident in his talent,
Poised on vacuity, framed Kao-t'ang—
Passed down for himself a name as shaper of rhapsodies;
Wild and wanton brought back Hsiang of Ch'u.
Now boldly embossed, the twelve peaks
Are cast forever as a weird and ghostly home.

The word here translated "vacuity" is the same that was transmogrified into "insubstantial" in my version of Li Po's double quatrain. Yü Fen is telling us that a human reputation and a magic mountain have been manufactured from very little substance. There is no respect for the goddess here.

Meng Chiao, who was a friend of Han Yü and whose literary style has been characterized as "anguished" and "odd," wrote two rather curious poems, one a sequel to the other, on the respectable *Wu shan kao* theme. The first, in seven-word lines, sets a gloomy prologue; the second, in quicker five-step beat, provides a dusky but happy finale. The scene opens among the twelve peaks of Shamanka Mountain, then shifts to the highland spot where the ancient king dreams alone. He is not shown walking with the poet Sung Yü as in the great tradition, but resting in the course of a hunting expedition; he dreams not by daylight but in the night. The goddess appears:

> Drifting mist, light and pink, moistens a ravishing form;
> Driving rain flies off and away—shining stars are few.

She disappears, and the ape voice of the king cries out in desolation. In the sequel the radiant vision is pursued with resolution—by whom? As the gibbon's cry fades away, the whispering rain becomes everything, concealing a lonely ghost. The soul of a king a thousand years dead finally achieves a second union: the damp fog congeals to form the doorway to a woman's chamber.[23] This is a little contrived and precious perhaps, but it is more dramatic than most elaborations on this common theme of satisfaction achieved after long separation and despair.

Li Ho wrote two poems about the bewitching strings of a shamanka's lute. The first, calling the goddess to the altar, is full of strange perfumes and disturbing shudders and chattering sounds. It has been translated more than once.[24] The other is a valediction, and shows the goddess leaving for her home on Wu shan. It is less eerie than the first one: the goddess is not so much ghostly as enticing—a witch who charms even the botanical world. Here then is "The Departure Song of Divine Strings":[25]

> The small woman of Shaman Mountain goes off
> > screened by clouds:
> The winds of spring shoot out pine flowerlets
> > on the mountain.
> Alone she pierces the green canopy—a fragrance heading
> > straight for home:
> A white horse and flowered pole go before—
> > thrusting and thrusting.
>
> The wind is mild on the Kiang in Shu, the water
> > like netted gauze—
> Yet who else could make sail on a fallen orchid
> > to cross over it?
> The cinnamon trees on a southern hill lie dead for
> > that lady
> Whose cloudy blouse is slightly stained from
> > pink pomade blossoms.

This poem has proved an embarrassment to commentators. It embarrasses me. My commentary will attempt to justify my translation:

> The rainbow goddess leaves the shamanka's altar,
> > darting through the clouds.
> Her ardent body bursts the pine catkins as she passes.

> She swoops up through the forest canopy, trailing
> sweet odors.
> She is preceded by a ceremonial steed, rigged with her
> flowery insignia.
>
> The great Yangtze by her home in the gorge is calm.
> Yet who will risk crossing it on a flower petal to meet
> her—only the goddess is capable of the feat.
> The evergreen cinnamons perish at her approach—the
> touch of the love goddess is dangerous.
> Her light shift is inevitably spotted with safflower,
> from which the rouge of courtesans is made.

Although Li Ho was singularly fond of botanical imagery, he did not feel bound to adhere to conventional and classical flower figures. Few of his poems lack some personal interpretation or some resurrected trope of a plant which often proves, when correctly understood, to be the key and crux of the poem's meaning. I cannot say with certainty that I have achieved the desired unlocking here.

The heartbreaking disappearance of the goddess leads by easy stages to the idea of the dissolution or death of the goddess. Will she return after a millennium to delight the ghost of the ancient king—or will she never return? The T'ang poets played infinite variations on this emotional enigma. It is not always absolutely clear whether they thought of the goddess as a vanished dream, a playful fantasy, or a symbol of an irrecoverable past. What, for instance, shall we make of Li Po's couplet:

> The divine woman's departure was long ago,
> Where now is King Hsiang to be found?[26]

Li Po's contemporary, the great minister and talented writer Chang Chiu-ling, is rather more explicit: the divine lovers are really gone forever:[27]

> Shaman Mountain comes close to the sky,
> A misted scene with a stretch of blue sparkle.
> Here it was that the King of Ch'u dreamed,
> Dreamed that he won the soul of the Divine Woman.
>
> The Divine Woman has long since gone away;
> Clouds and rain are gloomy, dark—and empty.
> Here is only the wail of the monkeys of Pa—
> No note of sorrow is to be heard.

Commentary:

> The high home of the goddess is close to heaven.
> Beneath her mists flows the glittering Yangtze.
> The archaic king met her here in a trance,
> And they were joined in mystical union.
>
> But that was long ago.
> Her aura of "clouds and rain" (amorous nostalgia)
>     remains—but she is not in them.
> The monkeys howl—but their crying is vain,
>     merely symbolic,
> Since the deserted grief-stricken king is long
>     dead and gone.

A similar effect is produced by different means in a composition of the ninth-century poet Li P'in. He sculls his boat through the choppy torrent and looks up at the magic mountain: after clear blue skies (in itself a token of the goddess's absence) there is some evening rain; the gibbon calls as usual:

> Once I heard that the divine woman has gone—
> Windblown bamboos sweep a vacant altar.[28]

The late ninth-century monk Ch'i-chi, a native of Ch'ang-sha but a wanderer, wrote many poems about the Hsiang River and its goddesses. He also did one on the *Wu shan kao* theme in which we find the king's spirit faded to the point of dissipation after the passage of centuries without the invigorating influence of love.[29] Here it is:

> The shaman mountain is high,
> The shaman woman uncanny:
> As rain, she brings the sunset, oh! as cloud,
>     she brings the dawn.
> The King of Ch'u is worn and haggard, his soul near
>     to extinction:
> An autumn gibbon bawls and howls—the sun goes on
>     to evening;
> Red-auroral clouds and purple mists clot
>     on the aging walls.
> A thousand cliffs, a myriad gullies, their flowers
>     all split open;
> But I feel that despite subtle fragrance they
>     lack the right colors.
> I cannot tell what travellers have gone this way in
>     past or present times:
> But have any men passed by this spot without
>     feelings of autumn?
> The clouds deepen, her temple is far—no use to
>     seek it out;
> The twelve peaks' tops pierce through to the deep blue
>     of the sky.

There is much that could be said about this spectral poem with its king gibbon slipping into the night, its off-color flowers, and its inaccessible shrine. But one thing that must be remarked on is the attention given by the poet to aural effects. The work begins with a bounce, as if we had in English:

> Shaman mountain feared,
> Shaman woman weird.

Or

> By shaman mountain daunted,
> By shaman woman haunted.

The same rhythm and rhyme are repeated in the next line, which is broken into equal and parallel halves by the archaic particle here translated "oh!". Then the smoothness is suddenly lost by a series of abrupt rhymes in -*k,* introducing a sharp, cranky note: *zyek* "evening," *pek* "wall," *t'yak* "split open," *sryek* "colors," *mek* "seek out," *pyek* "deep blue."

It is far from such chilling experiences as these to the re-creation of the goddess as a new kind of divinity, whether a neoclassical Taoist superwoman or a masked but mortal sweetheart.

An example of the former transformation—and it was not an uncommon one—appears, rather surprisingly, in a concoction by the famous court painter of the early T'ang period, Yen Li-pen. His skillfully contrived version of a familiar *yüeh fu* form opens with a conventional salutation-cum-question:[30]

> Lord, do you not see how Shaman Mountain, high
>     and haughty, rises half to heaven?
> Broken-off walls—a thousand fathoms—seemingly
>     painted there!
> Lord, do you not see how Shaman Mountain is circled
>     round where a turquoise screen opens?

It is the deep blue water of Hsiang and Kiang,
come to wind past that mount!

A theatrical opening: the curtain rolls up; then we tour
the whole setting of the stage: moonlit gorge, rising
clouds at daybreak, finally driving rain. There is even
the crying gibbon, the avatar of the King of Ch'u.
What is novel about this courtly pastiche is that the
goddess has been transformed into a finely boned, delicate sylphine creature who flies like a bird. Doubtless
she is privy to the alchemical secrets of Pao-p'u-tzu.
The old fertility deity has been superseded by a delicate, ethereal sky maiden, aloof from but not adverse
to the company of kings.

Another development was to present Jane Jones as
Aphrodite. Poets, either on their own initiative or in
response to polite request, did not find it hard to turn
out verses in which the women beloved by their friends
and patrons—especially at the time of some unhappy
separation—appear as goddesses visible, and their
lovers as latter-day sufferers of the very agonies that
had afflicted the King of Ch'u:

Light gown, jade girdle: she lingered, but
her stay was brief;
Late she went off with clouds and rain . . .[31]

This is a fragment of a poem written by Ch'üan Te-yü
for a friend who was suffering from the pangs of unful-
filled love. It presents the departed mistress in the
guise of the Divine Woman of Shamanka Mountain,
and the friend himself as a dejected king. Li Shang-yin
was good at this sort of thing, and it is not surprising to
encounter a couplet of his that displays a courtesan in

a magnate's suite drifting lightly in the gentle drizzle at Kao-t'ang, while the great man himself is figured as the ancient monarch, briefly delighted.[32]

Probably the most notorious of all deifying poets of the T'ang period—if so I may style those who were quick to turn a vamp into a Venus—was the uncontrollable Lo Ch'iu. This impulsive member of a famous literary trio of the last decades of decaying T'ang—he was related to Lo Yin and to Lo Yeh—was employed by Li Hsiao-kung, a provincial magnate. In this he was like many talented persons of an era when the imperial court could not offer the safety or comforts afforded by the tent of a warlord. One of the geisha of that lord's household was an enchanting person named Tu Hung-erh. Lo Ch'iu fell madly in love with her. But his employer intervened when the poet tried to gain the lady's favor with a rich gift—he had already promised her to a more exalted member of his staff. In a fit of jealous rage, Lo Ch'iu stabbed the charmer to death. The warlord condemned him for his crime, but Lo Ch'iu was lucky enough to escape death: a general amnesty was proclaimed just in time. Cooled down and remorseful, he set himself to the task of writing a sequence of a hundred odes to celebrate, as he states in his preface, the incomparable beauties of his victim, taking particular pains to match her with the most famous belles of classical literature.[33] Among those he rates highly are the Wu shan goddess and the Lo goddess, with their notorious witcheries. Sometimes they are only hinted at by means of allusions to "Shamanka Gorge" and "Lo River,"[34] but the penitent poet could also make a very direct identification, as when he writes that both the holy mountain and the holy river,

their old goddesses dead, were given new life by the reincarnation of their spirits in a lovely person from the
town of Tiao-yin—that is, in the person of Tu Hung-
erh:[35]

> Shamanka Mountain, Reach of Lo—in the beginning,
>     no feelings about them:
> That is all owed to a delightful person, and now
>     they have their fame.
> In our days, at Tiao-yin, there was divine loveliness;
> After us, no lordling will ever treat them lightly.

It was only a slight step further in the same direction to
identify the goddess, not with a beloved woman, but
with an entertainer personally unknown to the poet. It
was as if a European poet should attempt to immortal-
ize a celebrated nightclub dancer, rather than his own
mistress, by comparing her with Helen of Troy. Po
Chü-i did precisely this when he described a pair of
geisha from Chāch (modern Tashkent) in their exotic
belled hats and red shoes performing a frantic and passionate dance whose erotic nature is proven by the
poet's insertion of phrases from the Sung Yü poems.
These silver-belted aliens, then, were invested with the
native glamour of a divine seducer of Chinese kings.[36]

At the other extreme is the removal of the spirit of
Shamanka Mountain from real human affairs altogether, by transforming her into a mere type or standard metaphor. This was done, for example, in a *fu*
composed by Wang Ch'i, who was writing at the very
end of the T'ang period. It is a homily on good government cast in allegorical language, with the goddess
as a specious and almost incredible protagonist.[37] Fortunately the idea of diluting the image of the Divine

Woman to this extent did not attract many writers.

Finally, the ancient theme could even be treated in a jocular way. When a certain Yen Ching-ai visited the Kao-t'ang Inn in Hao-chou in the Huai region late in the T'ang period, he was inspired to write the following quatrain:

> I beg to ask "Where might King Hsiang be now?
> This place, with its hills and streams,
>      surpasses Yang-t'ai.
> If this evening he were to seek lodging in
>      Kao-t'ang Inn,
> Would the Divine Woman ever come into his dreams?"[38]

This rather silly poem contains a reminiscence of Po Chü-i's line in the *Ch'ang hen ko* which states that Hsüan Tsung, bereft of his consort, the lady Yang, had not even the consolation that her spirit "would ever come into his dreams." What it says is that the superb scenery in this modern Kao-t'ang, remote from the ancient site of that name, would certainly entrance the old King of Ch'u so much that his tranquilized mind would not even dream of a visit by the goddess for whom he had longed for so many centuries. Perhaps Yen Ching-ai was trying to flatter his landlord.


THE LO DIVINITY

The image of the Goddess of the Lo River in T'ang poetry is irreparably contaminated with Ts'ao Chih's courtly secularization of her in his *Lo shen fu*. Even the noble poet himself is presented in these latter-day compositions. Although in some of these literary works it is suggested that he is a kind of reincarnation of the charismatic King of Ch'u, the identification does not really come off, any more than do occasional vain attempts to invest the haughty goddess with some of the attributes of the Divine Woman of Shamanka Mountain. Once in a while a poet attempted to root her firmly in whatever supernatural overtones the name of the Lo River still retained from a more devout past, but what really gives life to the deity is that single literary tour de force of the third century. Li Chiao, for instance, attempted a catalogue of the more tradition- al mysteries associated with the river—a list vibrant with vermilion phoenixes and transcendental visitors and including even the venerable tortoise with the mystic chart displayed on its back. It comes as some- thing of a shock to find a very human Ts'ao Chih— referred to, as usual, as "Prince of Ch'en"—sharing the stage with these illustrious monsters:

The Prince of Ch'en stares at the ravishing person.[39]

But the majority of such references to the goddess show little deviation from a narrow set of conven- tions: she is a fleeting vision; she flutters over the waves; she is a fragile figure; her waist is slender; her socks are not wetted, and indeed the water is to her as is dust to a mortal woman; she can be detected by her perfume; she is tremulously white, like bleached silk, like a white lotus, like soft moonlight, like drifting snow:[40]

Past in a twinkling—a startled swan;
Quite gone away—a roving dragon![41]

But the dragon element in her is a mere convention— she is all too human. She is shown to her best advantage in a stanza by Li Shang-yin which combines several of these common motifs. He makes the most of her holy socks, which he imagines as lending the power to tread safely the watery surface of the moon:[42]

> Once I heard that Consort Fu's socks
> Crossing water almost got dusty.
> Delightful to borrow Ch'ang-o's garb,
> In the fresh of autumn to tread the moon's wheel!

Consort Fu, the anthropomorphized Lo goddess, here becomes the light-footed goddess of the moon. So she presides not only over an earthly river but also over its celestial counterpart—both were, as she was, exemplars of the *yin* principle. But Li Shang-yin has handled the ancient metaphysical belief as a mere literary conceit. The best that could be done with the figure of the wave treader was to insist on her as a model for geishas and court beauties. Yet she was outshone by a courtesan who lacked both the glitter of water surface and the sheen of moon. I refer to the fourteenth of Lo Ch'iu's poems in praise of the woman he had murdered. It says that if Ts'ao Chih could have glimpsed such a one as Hung-erh, he would not have emotions left to hymn the Spirit of the Lo.[43] In both cases the supernatural allusions are mere powder and rouge.

Hung-erh was a real though unique person. But the destiny of Consort Fu, even in her role as Goddess of the Lo, was depersonalization. She was compelled to stand for every handsome woman. Meng Hao-jan conjured up a vision of a lovely jadelike creature in whirling snow. Is she a living being or a spirit? It is not clear at first:

Her manner is like that of the spirit of the Lo River.[44]

But, even cloaked in fairy whiteness, she soon appears plainly as a coquettish aristocrat riding away down a real streamside path.

Wang Ch'i, whose unbecoming treatment of the Wu shan goddess has been alluded to, seems to have had little feeling for the divine. In a versified account of elite springtime picnics by the Ch'ü Chiang Lake in southeastern Ch'ang-an, among musicians and mountebanks, he shows a typical gallant of the town ogling a scented, moth-eyebrowed beauty who "from afar might even be the Person of the Reach of Lo."[45]

A welcome variation of the tedious theme has been provided us in a quatrain by Ch'üan Te-yü, a precocious writer and high offical at the end of the eighth century:

> Clouds and rain from Shaman Mountain:
>> the Lo River spirit!
> A beaded band on fragrant waist, securely fitted to body!
> She is desperate now, her makeup done—her lord
>> is not to be seen.
> Swallowing her feelings, she rises and stands,
>> and asks of a ferryman.[46]

To start: the goddess's image is fused with that of the Divine Woman. Then: the narrow waist of the incredible creature, excellent for either goddess or woman. In the end, it is simply a stricken woman, abandoning her dignity to ask a menial whether her lover is coming.

Despite such unusual treatment as this, we cannot say that the Lo Divinity inspired much original poetry.

In T'ang times, at least, the end result of Ts'ao Chih's efforts was the generation of a host of classical-cum-literary allusions—a Phyllis mask, a Chloe costume—which never evokes the awesome goddess of the crystal waters of an ancient river.

## THE HAN WOMAN

Of the famous river goddesses, the "Woman of the Han" fares least well as a literary figure. She never attains complete characterization. Beautiful, doubtless, but, except for her noble name, she lacks any specific trait to distinguish her. She seems to need a companion to provide a little borrowed luster, and so she is commonly found in company with one of the more fully developed water spirits, as in this *yüeh fu* quatrain by Yang Kuang, otherwise known as Sui Yang Ti:[47]

> Night dew enclosing breath of flowers;
> Spring tarn tremulous in moonlit dazzle.
> On Han Water one finds a roving woman;
> On Hsiang River one meets a pair of consorts.

Similarly Tu Fu, in a poem ostensibly in praise of a place noted for its handsome fish, has the Hsiang Consort and the Han Woman singing and dancing together, in company with alligators and whales in an electric atmosphere sparkling with divine presences.[48] Perhaps hyperbole is appropriate to great spirits of the water, but here one feels that the goddesses are being swamped by the flounderings of aquatic monsters.

Such double epiphanies as these do not, of course, always require the presence of the Han Woman, like the Holy Ghost, as the junior member of a sacred partnership. Another Tu Fu effusion about the lake district of northern Hunan couples the Hsiang Fairy with the ambiguous "Mountain Spirit" of the "Nine Songs," thought by some authorities to be none other than the Wu shan goddess.[49] It might be argued that in this case the Mountain Spirit had not yet in T'ang times been endowed with a specific identity, and accordingly that she too—if it was indeed a feminine spirit—might well profit from the supportive presence of the great lady of the south.

In a long rhapsodic treatment—replete with allegory—on the subject of gathering lotuses, Wang Po, the young genius of early T'ang, brings the same pair together. Indeed, it hardly seems just that in these florid phrases the purple waves of Lake Tung-t'ing and the green depths of the rivers Hsiao and Hsiang are marked as the center and focus of the water world, while the venerable Han is diminished to a minor tributary. At any rate, Wang Po invigorates his water plants by means of allusions to lovely but probably not willowy ladies, even comparing the pink-tinged lotus to lovely faces flushed by wine. We are not surprised to find, in this welter of classical streams and strolling belles, both the Woman of Han and the Fairy of Hsiang.[50] One other poet observed the hue of a pink flower in the cheeks of the Han sprite—but it is an artificial color. He was Li Ch'ün-yü, author of so many poems about Lake Tung-t'ing, the River Hsiang, and the famous and fashionable naiads that haunted them. In a sensuous composition on the movement, colors, and subtle odors of roses, he confesses that the sight of one such flower by the water's edge is "like a glimpse of the makeup of the Han Woman."[51] Not a great concession perhaps, although some flower fanciers might be pleased to find a gentle rose among so many full-blown lotuses.

The Han Woman was elevated at least once above mere simpering ballroom blushes to enjoy a moderate success as a natural force, like one of Dr. Darwin's scientific nymphs. This was in a poem, by Ku K'uang, which holds the authorities of the Dragon Palace strangely innocent of the ravages caused by a devastating flood of the lower Kiang in the seventies of the eighth century. As the great river tumbles violently toward the sea, the kraken mermaids, apparently drifting up from the salty estuary, find themselves weaving thread from fresh-water lotuses into their precious sea fabrics, while, as the dragon's reservoirs are depleted, a surprising meeting takes place in the uncontrollable wash:

> Han Woman and Kiang Consort follow gloomily,
>     one after the other.[52]

### THE HSIANG CONSORT

Probably it was inevitable that the Hsiang Goddess should compose her own lament on the death of her noble husband. In a register of the titles of ancient tunes for the zither, the Sung monk Chü-yüeh lists, among the compositions of high antiquity, a "Plaint of the Hsiang Consort" *(Hsiang fei yüan),* the supposed work of Maiden Bloom.[53] Moreover "The Book of T'ang" lists the same title in its monograph on ritual as number 23 among twenty-four tunes for an orchestra of wind and percussion instruments.[54] Presumably the goddess did not orchestrate this version of her complaint. In any event, even without surviving examples, it would not have been hard to surmise the content of the songs that were sung to the tune—if it *was* only a single tune. In the T'ang poems bearing this title, the "complaint" is the common one of the neglected wife or mistress, for whom the Hsiang goddess provides a lovely disguise. Her perennial tears and the bamboos they stain forever are all too common stereotypes of the weeping of any slighted, deserted, or widowed woman of the elite class. The interested reader may find an example from the pen of Meng Chiao, who was singularly devoted to this theme and others like it, in a recent volume of translations of late T'ang poetry.[55] Another example is provided by one of the two poems entitled *Hsiang fei yüan* written by the early ninth-century poet and court official Ch'en Yü:[56]

> There where the Two Consorts complain the clouds
> > make a thick veil;
> There where the Two Consorts lament the Hsiang
> > waters are deep.
> An itinerant merchant's wine dribbles on the grass
> > before their shrine:
> Sighing, soughing, the wind rises in their thicket of
> > spotted bamboo.

It appears that the unloved salesman has desecrated a holy spot, and the rising wind is the indignant sighing of the ancient spirits, especially the spirit of King Hsiang of Ch'u. But at least the unintentional libation has revived a dying ghost. The "wind as king" image is common enough. We see it again in a poem by Hsü Hun, a provincial magistrate who lived somewhat later in the ninth century. After hearing a performance of the old lament on a stringed instrument, he writes, as the last verse of an octet:

> The wind raises the cold waves — the sun presses
>     into twilight.[57]

But beyond those extant poems bearing the traditional title there is a host of others, published under a great variety of captions but with style and content of the same sort. Some are good poems whose occasion was a rather trivial event; others are mediocre poems attempting to be solemn. All intermediate gradations occur as well. "Yao's daughter weeping in Ts'ang-wu"[58] may occur simply as one of a number of allusions to local sights and celebrities thought to be appropriate to embellish a few verses demonstrating the correct emotions during a visit to Lake Tung-t'ing. The Consort of the Hsiang may weep, and hosts of lesser spirits may be stupefied by such tribute from aristocratic writers, as in a flattering sequence written by Tu Fu in Hunan.[59] Appropriate allusions to the Temple of the Two Consorts, to the Peaks of Nine Uncertainties, and even to a thwarted dragon occur in a poem meant to console a fellow official en route into a barbarous southern wilderness.[60] The consolation seems small enough. Even the inimitable Li Ho falters when, in a rather sentimental poem that is full of popular images (dew, moon, bamboos, and so on) but rather contrived and inconsequential, he repeats the conventional theme of a lonely woman in the guise of the Hsiang goddess:

The play of water—girdle ornaments of the
  Hsiang Fairy.[61]

The lady receives more serious treatment from the pen
of Sun Ti, a writer with an excellent sense of the fitting
word, who enjoys much less repute in our times than
the three poets just referred to. He seems to have been
keen on boating and composed many verses about the
Yangtze and other waterways. In one delightful vision
his little craft, traversing the Dragon Rapids, seems to
yearn for the underwater pavilions of the gods where
"The Consort of the Kiang dances in her halcyon-blue
room."[62] Sun Ti's eighth-century contemporary,
Chang Chiu-ling, wrote many poems about the Hsiang River which have the distinction of ignoring the
legend of Shun altogether and showing a true regard
for unadorned nature. In his case, however, the Hsiang flowed away from his southern homeland, and so
it was not for him a bookish region as it was for many
other T'ang poets.

The monumental Ch'ing anthology *T'u shu chi
ch'eng* contains a large repertory of poems about Lake
Tung-t'ing and the rivers that feed its depths. This collection affords us an easy survey of poems on this subject and includes examples by such eminent writers as
Chang Yüeh, Li Po, Tu Fu, and Han Yü.[63] Although,
unlike Chang Chiu-ling, these poets had not known the
warm lands of the south as childhood playgrounds,
they did, often enough, take some account of their delightful scenery. Naturally, they also reacted to the
numinous nature of the lake. Fishy, draconic creatures
frequently figure in their efforts. But most of all it was

the thought that this was the heartland of the romantic old state of Ch'u that made their hearts flutter. Here the great king walked! Here the amorous goddess, now remembered more as an ancient queen than as a real deity, manifested herself to a chosen few.

It comes as no surprise, then, that in many poems about the lake region and its reigning spirits the Hsiang Consort assumes the attributes of the Divine Woman of Shamanka Mountain. Both, after all, were classical goddesses of Ch'u—obvious equivalents, like Venus and Aphrodite. In the ninth century, Chu Ch'ing-yü, admiring Lake Tung-t'ing with the assistance of a flagon of wine, wrote:

> Sailing up from Pa-ling, passing by her hill:
> Rain goes with the Divine Woman, coming from
>     the gorge's verge.[64]

Here the Wu shan woman, floating damply toward the lake, assumes the guise of her alter ego. At about the same time, Li Ch'ün-yü, that antisocial man and variable poet, wrote of the twinned Hsiang goddess at her holy isle in the lake, "Whirling, whirling in the midst of mist and rain."[65] She is a clear metamorphosis of her sister from upstream. A similar and contemporary example comes to us from the brush of Liu Yü-hsi. The unstable identity of the two goddesses is not so obvious here, but no great wisdom is needed to detect it:[66]

> Hsiang Water flow!
> Hsiang Water flow!
> Nine Doubts' cloudy beings are despondent still.
> You ask, milord, "At what place are the
>     Two Consorts staying?"
> With the perfumed herbs of Ling-ling, amidst the dew,
>     in autumn!

This *yüeh fu* survives in a number of variant forms; one substitutes "rain" for "dew," and so on. If "dew" is used, the writer's intent is plain: it is a common symbol of tears, and goes naturally with "autumn," the season of pain. "Rain," on the other hand, would refer obviously to the Divine Woman—but we need not feel compelled to prefer the word. If the Divine Woman is here at all, she is disguised more subtly as "dew." In any event, the locale is the less usual one of the headwaters of the Hsiang, in the county of Ling-ling, whose sweet basil was famous in east Asia. Here the odor of the herb represents the sweet scent of the goddess herself.

It is an easy next step to make the goddess—or goddesses—into drifting riverside ghosts:

We cannot tell where your subtle, residual
    soul wanders—
But the falling sun on Hsiao and Hsiang hollows
    the white clouds.[67]

This couplet from a poem by Hu Tseng, who wrote in the tent courts of provincial warlords late in the ninth century, pictures the goddess as a lingering earthbound spirit, no different from any ghost yielded up by a human being. She floats cloudlike above her rivers, vulnerable and transparent to the brilliant rays of the setting sun. Perhaps these transfixing shafts of light represent the divine virility of the great Shun flashing through the evening sky.

More conventional evocations of the Hsiang goddess demand material attributes, comparable to the artifacts in the hands of Lakshmi or Kali. One such convention requires that the goddess should, if possible, play the *se*, a large antique zither, its true classical form long since forgotten. The allusion can turn up almost anywhere if a classical sound is required—as when Wu Jung, poeticizing fancifully about various sights and sounds, introduces "the zither of Yao's daughter" as the most lovely of stringed instruments, rather like Orpheus' lyre.[68] Similarly, Tu Fu, in an ekphrasis in praise of landscape painting, mentions the spotted bamboos in a moist, dreamlike setting along riverbanks populated by ghostly presences, but notes the absence of the Hsiang Consort and her marvelous cittern.[69]

As has already become apparent, the elegant maculated bamboos themselves are probably the most commonly demanded props in poetic re-creations of the drama of Shun and his wives. The ladies' tears— they must be bloody tears in order to stain the bamboo stems—occur everywhere in the poetry of the Six Dynasties and T'ang. Their presence, sometimes unfairly, is liable to provoke yawns from the reader. Like perennially weeping willows, they do not appeal to our age, however much they may have inspired sensibility in early medieval China. Nevertheless, occasionally the cliché suggested a fine figure of speech, notably in the writings of ninth-century poets, where they often become metaphors twice-removed. For Tu Mu, the bamboo stems show more than traces of divine tears:

Blood-dyed, spot on spot—to form damask pattern.[70]

The image of a damask weave with repeated red medallions (a live enough allusion in T'ang times) was occasioned merely by the poet's contemplation of the handle of his writing brush, fashioned from a piece of the celebrated plant. Wen T'ing-yün goes even further.

In a quatrain on the subject of a woman's hair orna-
ment set with blue gemstones—presumably lapis lazu-
li or sapphire—he transforms the jewels into streams
of water-blue tears pouring down the cheeks of the antique water woman:

Halcyon-dyed, ethereal as ice, translucent as dew.[71]

Here the bamboo does not even appear. Nor does it in
a line by P'i Jih-hsiu which compares the pink seeds of
a pomegranate to the bloodied tears of the Consort of
the Hsiang.[72] (P'i Jih-hsiu was fond of these botanical
metaphors—more imagistic and less symbolic than
those of Li Ho—as when he makes a mermaid figure
out of the Hsiang Consort to provide an occasion on
which to hang some drifting duckweed, "tender as
gold ointment," transmuted into the nymph's filigree
hair jewel.)[73] Abandoning the all-too-familiar tears altogether, Li Hsien-yung, in an elaborate fantasy based
on the gift of a package of tea from a friendly monk,
imagined that he saw the greenish hair of the Hsiang
Fairy swirling in his bowl as he mixed the powdered
tea leaves.[74] Even more fantastic, possibly, is the transformation—effected by more than one T'ang poet—of
a strange rock, apparently well known to sightseers of
the eighth century: it yielded the hallucinatory figure
of a woman looking for her lost husband. Her figure is
clothed in green mosses and lichens, as in an ancient
robe, and the dew that spangles its surface is—of
course—the eternal tears of the petrified goddess.[75]

We are fortunate in having a poem composed by the
Hsiang goddess herself, or perhaps by some lesser sister. In the official T'ang anthology there is a poem
whose author is identified simply as "Maiden in the

Midst of the Hsiang."[76] This ghost poem was recited for a certain minister Cheng when he was traveling in Hunan, and it may be that it is the work of a real hetaira, assuming the mantle of the goddess in order to tell the good minister that their brief affair, enhanced with wine and music through an autumn night, is forever over:

> That red tree—the color of intoxication in autumn;
> That blue stream—a string strummed at night.
> A delightful meeting that may not be repeated:
> This wind and rain are blurring them—as will the years.

We have come a long way from the river goddess in her simple dragon nature. Like the lovely creature by the river, her antique form has been blurred by the passage of time. But it was not entirely forgotten in T'ang times. Characteristically, the fantast Li Ho was one of those who remembered it. In his "Song Simulating a Dragon's Chant," a rather pleasant pastiche full not only of dragons but of goddesses and numinous birds, he takes special account of the Lady of the Kiang.[77] The presence of the birds is worth noting. Dragons, birds, and our goddesses are all creatures that fly through the clouds. The name "Divine Woman," given to the Wu shan goddess, reminds us of the name "Heavenly Woman," which applies with equal propriety to a goddess and to the magpie who announces the approach of storms.[78] Furthermore it is said that the Hsiang goddesses, as daughters of Yao, taught their beloved Shun the art of flying like a bird.[79] Numinous bird and divine reptile are the same. Pterodactyl and Archaeopteryx are one.

In the "Nine Songs," the lady of the Hsiang also appears under the alias of "God's Child" *(ti tzu):*

God's Child descends, oh! to North Holm!

Medieval poets naturally accepted the equivalence, and God's Child appears with monotonous regularity in verses celebrating the supernatural aspects of the central lake region. Li Po, notoriously susceptible to spirit women, referred to her more than once under her sobriquet; for instance:

God's Child weeps, oh! among the green clouds.
Away with wind and waves, oh! gone beyond return.[80]

The message here is the usual one, but the language imitates that of the "Nine Songs." I like to think that the unusual "green clouds" are the clouds that flow through the wet sky of an underwater realm. An even more striking display of colors illuminates the young goddess's domain in this quatrain, also by Li Po. It is the second of a set of five about Lake Tung-t'ing:

God's Child has gone from Hsiao and Hsiang,
        not to return.
Void and vacant the autumn herbs amid Tung-t'ing.
But, palely tinted on shining lake, displayed
        as in a jade mirror,
Painted out in vermilion and blue: there is
        Chün shan![81]

The goddess herself has vanished, as often, but her holy island in the lake with its handsome shrine remains to represent her and to remind us of the possibility of her eventual return. Still, there are no bright new ideas here.

Less well centered in the mainstream of literary tradition, and therefore more interesting, is a long shamanistic poem written by Li Po's contemporary, Li Chia-yu, on the occasion of witnessing a household ritual in the wild country south of the Kiang. He begins by noting the relationship between the simple religious ceremonies of the south in his own days and those which could be deduced from the content of the ancient poems of Ch'u.[82] In an atmosphere redolent of the classical sacrificial wine, which was flavored with the potent carpels and seeds of fagara,[83] God's Child skims the banks of the Hsiang.[84] The reader is reminded of Li Ho's shamanka poems. There is some of the same primitive flavor in a quatrain from the pen of the painter and calligrapher Ku K'uang—noted also for his well-developed sense of humor. Although such normal motifs as Tung-t'ing Lake, the cloudy soul of the King of Ch'u, the bamboo thickets, and the heart-rending cry of the gibbon—the king's ghostly voice—all appear, the lines hint at shamanistic rites, with Szechwanese believers chanting in the darkness:[85]

> God's Child will not return to Ts'ang-wu again.
> At Tung-t'ing leaves fall, a cloud from Ch'u
> is flying.
> The men of Pa sing by night behind the bamboo
> branches.
> But the bowel-tearing gibbon's voice is more and more
> rare at dawn.

The ancient king, left desolate at dawn, is fading away like an ancient picture or the memory of a song. The goddess herself becomes pale and devitalized. Li Ch'ün-yü writes comparably in one of his many verses on the watery southern lands. He points to the Shrine of God's Child amid the fragrant flowers of spring, but

> These bygone things, separated from us by the years,
> are like dreams that pass us by.[86]

Once again, then, we are in the presence of phantoms. In A.D. 751, Ch'ien Ch'i set himself to compose a poem full of tinkling sounds and sweet odors on the subject of the Hsiang spirit, whom he addresses as "God's Child," performing on the archaic zither. The previous year he had been staying in a hostel in the lake district. One night he heard a mysterious voice chanting in the courtyard:

> The song is over—no person can be seen;
> Above the Kiang a number of peaks show blue.

Now later, as he pondered the right words for his treatment of the sacred subject, he found it inevitable that this spectre-given couplet serve as the conclusion of his own poem.[87]

All of this preliminary material about God's Child is merely a prologue to a consideration of her incredible sex change in a T'ang poem of great repute. Well before T'ang times, God's Child had become firmly established as the junior miss of the divine pair—somewhat more appealing and daintily feminine than her elder sister. It comes as something of a shock to find her transmogrified into a very human male in most— perhaps all—modern interpretations of a haunting, elusive, and dangerously deceptive poem by the precocious Wang Po. The celebrated composition has been much translated. The translators have all done both

the author and the goddess a disservice. They uniformly accept the verdict of the modern Chinese critics,
namely that the expression "God's Child" must, in
Wang Po's poem, be rendered "le jeune roi," "der
junge König," "royal builder," "emperor's son."
Why? Only because the occasion of the poem was the
renovation and rededication of a riverside pleasure
house built earlier by a member of the royal house of
T'ang. The interested reader may wish to look into the
history of the misinterpretation, by insensitive but ingenious interpreters, of this ode as addressed not to the
Hsiang goddess but to the high-born prince.[88] Here,
however, is a translation, feeble as it may be as literature, which attempts to present something of the
poem's real meaning. This requires the identification
of its central figure, in the obvious and traditional
way, as the goddess herself.

> The high gallery of the Prince of T'eng
>     looked out on a holm in the Kiang.
> There girdle gems and ringing bells marked the end
>     of song and dance.
> At dawn, painted beams flew out against the clouds
>     from South Reach.
> At dusk, pearly curtains rolled up towards
>     the rain on West Hill.
>
> Now idle clouds are images in pools, and those days
>     remote and hazy.
> All things are altered, the stars shifted,
>     many autumns meted out.
>
> Inside the gallery—is God's Child now
>     to be found there?
> She is outside its railing, where the long Kiang
>     flows, vacant and indifferent!

The words here translated "reach" *(p'u)* and "holm" *(chu)* form part of the standard repertory of references to the goddess's holy island in Lake Tung-t'ing, here fancifully transferred further down the great river which was also part of her domain, and poems about her use them repeatedly. The crucial phrase "Where is God's Child now?" or—as I have just put it "is God's Child now to be found there?"—has echoes in many T'ang poems, which always refer to a great river goddess. In the seventh century an austere scholar named Yang Chiung referred to the goddess of Shamanka Mountain in virtually identical terms: "Where is the Lovely Person now?"[89] And in the eighth century Liu Ch'ang-ch'ing, in his quatrain "Hsiang Consort," wrote "God's Child may not be seen."[90] Whatever they may appear to be when turned into English, all of these are very simple variants of the same classical phrase in Chinese. Wang Po's very line, unaltered in any detail, appears again in a tribute, written in the eighth century by Ma Huai-su, to the "Gold City Princess," sent off to marry an unworthy Tibetan king, just as the Lady of the Hsiang had been compelled to accompany Shun into the savage southern wilderness.[91] Let us hope that, although the lovely image of God's Child may rightly conjure up visions of seductive female favorites in a pleasure house by the Kiang, Wang Po would never have used it to refer to the house's princely owner. Let this East Asian Ozymandias be exorcized forever! In any event, the goddess was indifferent to him.

# 4 The Goddess Epiphanies of Li Ho

Shut up from pleasure in a holy fountain,
A nymph lies, hearing the woollen water . . .
She longs, she longs, but no one calls to her.
In lapidary totals go the water-woken syllables.

*Lawrence Durrell*
"The Hive of Innocence," from Sappho

It was Li Ho who took it upon himself to oppose the tendency to secularize the water goddesses and to humanize the dragon women of antiquity.

Because Li Ho is now at last in vogue, it would be pointless here to recapitulate the meager details of his biography,[1] to refine appreciations of his writings, or even to attempt a superficial survey of his poetic work. Efforts at achieving all of these aims have already appeared in many languages. Rather I shall concentrate on only one aspect of his genius, which has so recently come to be appreciated after the neglect, misunderstanding, or obloquy of centuries of critics who were blind equally to his love of ancient goddesses and to his gift for exploiting the rich resources of his language. The dour and puritanical judges of the post-Sung era interpreted and dismissed both subject and treatment as mere frivolity.[2]

Li Ho's interest in this subject was not unrelated to his linguistic preferences. If he rejoiced in dark thoughts about divine apparitions, it was partly because these personae gave him rich opportunities to indulge his preferences for particular color words. He liked those related to the blue-green part of the spectrum, and also white, the color of metal, of death, of specters, of stark dreamworlds. It is curious that the climax of his preoccupation with the divine world came during the last year of his life, during and after his return to his home from the capital—a time when, renewing the *Ch'u tz'u* tradition, he wrote his poems "Hsiang Consort," "Shaman Mountain is High," and "Lady of Cowrie Palace."[3] This set forms a subdivision of the class of bizarre and supernatural themes that make up a large part of his surviving verse— poems full of bogles, shamankas, haunted animals, enchantments, nightmares, and frightful atmospheres. Long after his death it was usual for critics to write of his "talent for specters."[4] Accordingly, he loved the ancient poems of Ch'u and the divine water women that inhabited them.

The shamanistic tone of much of his work, evident both in his goddess poems and in those plainly labeled as shaman songs (for instance, the pair of "Divine Strings" poems)[5] is due not only to Li Ho's love of the *Ch'u tz'u*, but to the influence on him of the old *yüeh fu* songs, particularly those made in the Wu area during the early part of the Six Dynasties period.[6] But it seems almost ludicrous to speak of "influence" on Li Ho. These same ancient songs "influenced" other T'ang poets. But there is a wide difference between, on the one hand, borrowing classical themes as good, reliable stereotypes or capturing brilliant images to convert to one's secondary purposes, and, on the other hand, taking a personal treasured image and renovating it completely—making it blossom, as it were, for the first time. What Shakespeare did to Italian stories is what Li Ho did to the shaman songs. Although his poems drew on the past, he was the opposite of an imitator—he was a highly original creator. If he resorted to the linguistic imagery of those old poems, he did not fail to reorchestrate them and so to transform them into something entirely his own. Compare Brahms, "Variations on a Theme by Haydn." There is nothing pedantic, familiar, or "archaistic" about his re-creations.

Indeed, some of Li Ho's water women have no obvious classical antecedents; they are as fresh as if born yesterday. They are Li Ho's own artifacts, suggested perhaps by a phrase in one of the old rhapsodies. These new evocations carry an almost overwhelming conviction of the reality of the divine beings they describe. These are no conventional deities, nor are they usually flattering masks for popular courtesans, as in the manner of so many of his contemporaries. They are truly strange, inhuman, and—except for Li Ho's talent—ineffable. The poet somehow manages to express their remoteness from all normal experience. In a sense, he is himself a possessed shaman, describing his vision of a unique supernatural protectress. His language is not the hysterical chant of a shaman, however, but elegantly phrased in the most difficult and fantastic imagery. At the same time, he reveals himself as the mortal lover of an immortal being, who is ultimately unattainable.[7] He was trying passionately to revivify and actualize a dream of beauty and to demonstrate his devotion to a quasi-religious ideal—an ambition quite out of step with the literary life of his times, when the ancient goddesses could only be fossilized relics or trite topics for the amorously inclined. Li Ho at least could breathe life into their faded figures—an unparalleled achievement for a Chinese mythographer. Li Ho was, on a particularly magnificent scale, in the class of the "enamored" bards of Turkey, who put their mystical visions of beloved women, whom they sought diligently in the real world, to words and music.[8] These poets followed an ancient shamanistic tradition in using a syllabic kind of verse, ignoring the quantitative rules followed by the Ottoman court poets. But they were closer to folk poetry than Li Ho was to the popular poets who stood behind the *yüeh fu*.

I am compelled to disagree in part with Professor Hawkes who, while acknowledging the brilliance of Li Ho's semi-erotic fantasies, takes pains to state that the poet did not "believe" in the divine figures he evoked.[9] He must, in my view, have believed in them in some sense in order to infuse such vivid life in them. While adhering to the opinion that a good poet is primarily a linguistic craftsman—a creator of word artifacts—I cannot help finding something of the magician and the priest in Li Ho. I am convinced that he believed in the ultimate reality of his own re-creations: for him, in *some* magic world, the goddesses existed.

Li Ho seems to have been entranced with the sounds of words more than most of his better-known contemporaries. It is not my intention here to analyze this aspect of his poetry in any detail, but simply to take note of a fact that needs much more study. Because Professor Pulleyblank has elucidated them for us,[10] we can now hear the rhymes of Li Ho's verses much as men of the ninth century heard them, without having them filtered through the early seventh-century phonology reconstructed by Professor Karlgren. However, I suspect that Li Ho may sometimes have adhered to rhyme tables that represented speech already out of use in his own times. For instance, although the rhymes of "The Departure Song of the Divine Strings" are clear only in terms of Pulleyblank's ninth-century reconstructions, the rhymes of "The Song of God's Child" follow *Ch'ieh yün* categories exactly. Pulleyblank's labors also help to vivify imitative effects, such as the ringing metallic sonorities of "Lady of Cowrie Palace" in the second and fourth positions (immediately before the caesura) and in "The Departure Song of the Divine Strings" before the caesura.

Possibly the best resumé—admittedly an impressionistic one—of the power of Li Ho's words is an encomium attributed to his older friend, Han Yü:[11]

> The unbroken filiations of clouds and smoke are not up to their manner;
> The profound remoteness of the waters is not up to their passion;
> The brim-fullness of spring is not up to their harmonies;
> The clear purity of autumn is not up to their style;

A mast in the wind or a horse in battle line is not up to
their boldness;

Tile and coffin, seal and cauldron are not up to their antiquity;

Flowers in season and beautiful women are not up to their
color;

Wasted nations, ruined basilicas, thorns and brush, hill-
ocks and dunes are not up to their indignation, their
animosity, their sorrow, and their misery;

The sucking of the whale, the leaping of the giant turtle,
the ox demon, the snake god are not up to their desolation, their wildness, their distortions and their illusions.

But it is time to turn directly to some of these poems.

Li Ho could hardly have neglected the most powerful and persistent of the ancient river goddesses, the
goddess of the Hsiang, whose sway also extended up
and down the Yangtze for an indeterminate distance.
She was also sometimes identified, as in a prose story
that we shall note presently, with the venerable goddess of the Lo, and with the goddess of Wu shan. So
much has already become clear: she had become the
mistress of all of the waters of Central China. Like
many of his poems, Li Ho's "Hsiang Consort"[12] is
knotty, intricate, and almost untranslatable because of
its complex allusions and uncompromising reliance on
metaphor. A commentary is essential. But first the
basic poem:

Spotted bamboo of a thousand years—aging but undying.
Long companying the houri of Ch'in—a canopy on
Hsiang Water.
The incantations and provocations of the maids
of the Man fill the chilly void.

The Nine Mountains — unmoving green;
  the tear flowers — red.

A parted simurgh, a separated phoenix, she —
  deep in misty Ts'ang-wu.
Like cloud of Wu and rain of Shu — communion achieved
  from afar.
While dark and dismal the autumn breath ascends
  the blue-green sweetgums
In cool night — among the waves — she enchants
  that ancient dragon.

And now a short explication:

Since the death of Shun, the tear-spotted bamboos have
  survived the centuries.
The bamboos, like the spirit of the goddess ("houri of
  Ch'in"), have long hovered over the river.
The aboriginal ("Man") shamankas still mourn for Shun;
  they try to lure him back with their spells.
"The Nine Mountains" are the supposed burial place of
  Shun, carpeted with evergreen vegetation, spotted by
  the goddess's tears.

The goddess is a divine bird, parted from her mate in the
  humid forest of subtropical Ts'ang-wu.
"Cloud of Wu" is the mist goddess of Wu shan; "Rain of
  Shu" is the impregnating spirit of her lover, the king
  of Ch'u, come from afar to join her. They are here
  identified with the Hsiang goddess and her lover
  Shun.
Even the breath of autumn — cold, sad, and deadly —
  forces the sap up into the liquidambar trees which
  symbolize the divine king.
In the river the bull alligator — king, rain summoner, ancient dragon — is invigorated by the chant of the
  shamanka who impersonates the goddess mistress.

Compare with *ku lung* "ancient dragon" as a phonetic transcription of Cambodian *kurung* "king."

In another poem, "Song of God's Child,"[13] Li Ho has celebrated the goddess of the Hsiang under the alternate title given her in the "Nine Songs." The reader will also recognize allusions to Wang Po's famous ode on the gallery of the Prince of T'eng, both in the use of the term *ti tzu* "god's child" and in the reference in both to the old *yüeh fu* "Young Gentleman of the White Rock":

The Gentleman of White Rock dwells by the Kiang,
Guided before by the Sire of the Kiang, followed
behind by fishes.[14]

"Dwells by the Kiang" (which could just as well be "dwells overlooking the Kiang") becomes "looked out on a holm in the Kiang" in Wang Po's masterpiece; in Li Ho's transmutation, the phrase is merely suggested by the reference to the mysterious esquire. But beyond the classical allusions, the poem teems with ghostly lights, alarming cries, and supernatural vapors. It goes like this:

God's Child from Tung-t'ing—a thousand miles.
Cool winds, a wild goose cry—sky lies on water.
Nine-jointed sweet flags die on the stones.
The Hsiang Deity strums a zither—invites God's Child.

In aged cinnamons on the hill's crest old
aromatics alter.
A woman dragon chants plaintively—
cold water lights up.
The fish run by sandy reach: it is the
Gentleman of White Rock!

Lazily he takes a true pearl—hurls it into the
    dragon hall.

In this complicated poem the goddess calls to her
counterpart, a river god (under the old name of Young
Gentleman of White Rock), possibly represented by a
shaman. Here is a line-by-line commentary:

The Hsiang goddess can fly out a thousand miles from her
    headquarters in Lake Tung-t'ing.
The call of a goose in the cool autumn air passes over the
    sky-reflecting lake: she is in flight!
Wild plants shrivel on lakeside stones at the touch of the
    cold divine presence.
Her sister calls to her with the sound of music. Or is it a
    male deity?

Cinnamon wood matures—the sacred odor of the south-
    land.
The dragon lady is the goddess in her serpentine form—
    she calls for her mate.
He appears as a mysterious figure from a folk poem,
But he is contemptuous: a dragon pearl is his for the ask-
    ing, but he tosses it back.

This fantasy is a translation into medieval terms of the
mood of the old shaman poems of the "Nine Songs,"
in which the pleading shaman is left hopeless. But here
Li Ho reverses the roles of lover and beloved. The
white rock man is the alter ego of Shun: unexpectedly
he disdains the divine pearl—his ages-old dragon wife.

It is necessary to mention in passing a poem in
which Li Ho alludes not to one but to many supernatural figures, among whom are the Hsiang Consort, in
her inflated guise as "houri of the Kiang," and Nü
Kua. Both, cloaked in appropriate imagery, appear in

his paean to the famous harper Li P'ing,[15] whose music had power over the worlds of men and gods alike. Although the poem celebrates primarily the magical talent of a virtuoso musician—and Li Ho was fascinated by music—it is laden with images characteristic of his goddess poems—cold, white, metallic, draconic, and watery. In these verses there is the full diapason: autumn, towering clouds, the White-silk Woman (another goddess), jade, lotus, dew, "cool light," stars, Nü Kua's stones, rain, krakens, moon, dampness. A typical line describes the cumulus clouds frozen in place by the divine energy of the harp strings:

The void is white with clotted clouds, sprawled
and driftless.

But here now is an attempt to put a poem devoted to a single goddess, the "Lady of Cowrie Palace," into English. Ultimately it is a hopeless task, because the T'ang original rings with metallic sounds that cannot be transferred to English from Chinese. The multiple allusions and double images, too, can only be hinted at. Some European cognates may serve as a fanfare or eye-opening prelude to Li Ho's presentation of the aqueous domain and palatial residence of an immortal queen, both more icy and free of passion than the Snow Queen of Hans Christian Andersen and her frosty palace. Li Ho conjures up a vivid picture of a frozen, immobile, ageless, silvery, petrified, static, metallic, crystalline being. The goddess is deathless; she fears no change nor corruption—and can share nothing with a mortal creature. There are intimations of the mineral immortality of such a creature in our own literary heritage. Erasmus Darwin, for instance, the bard of triumphant science, wrote of her:

> Call from her crystal cave the Naiad Nymph,
> Who hides her fine form in the passing lymph.[16]

But this nymph is an artificial nymph—a nymph of the head, not of the heart. Then there is the nymph of the soul and religious fantasy, not unknown to William Blake:

> But silken nets and traps of adamant
>     with Oothoon spread,
> And catch for thee girls of mild silver,
>     or of furious gold.[17]

Others of the breed would not have astonished Li Ho, however. One such is the unlucky heroine of the fairy story "Undine," written by Friedrich Baron de la Motte-Fouqué:

> . . . in den Seen und Strömen und Bächen lebt der Wasser-geister ausgebreitetes Geschlecht. In klingenden Krystall-gewölben, durch die der Himmel mit Sonn' und Sternen hereinsieht, wohnt sich's schön; hohe Korallenbäume mit blau und roten Früchten leuchten in den Gärten; über reinlichen Meeressand wandelt man, und über schöne bunte Muscheln, und was die alte Welt des also Schönen besass, dass die heutige nicht mehr sich dran zu freuen würdig ist, das überzogen die Fluten mit ihren heimlichen Silberschleiern . . .

And so on. Just so was the shelly palace of the god of the Yellow River, the crystalline habitat of the Chinese ondines—cold, beautiful, ophidian nixies.

These frigid creatures have a long and lively history in Chinese literature. Sometimes they resemble the adamantine fairies and silvery sylphs of Taoist mythology, "whose flesh and skin resemble ice and snow";[18] sometimes they are like the "jade women" of Li Po's vision of T'ai shan, the sacred mountain.[19] Above all, the elegant Ch'an monk, Kuan-hsiu, who illuminated the court of Shu in the tenth century, was conscious of the mineral nature of transcendent beings such as these: "The entities which populate this dreamland are realized stalactites, coagulated salts, or gems crystallized out of the primordial magma."[20] (The words are my own, commenting on Kuan-hsiu's remarkable paradise poems.) But despite these very respectable antecedents and analogues, no goddess of jade was ever realized so brilliantly as Li Ho's "Lady of Cowrie Palace."[21] It is a poem of a kind rare not only in Chinese literature, but in world literature:

> Clink! clink! the Lake Woman toys with metal bangles.
> A birdlike headpiece—cocked tail, folded wings.
> In her six palaces there is no speech—all life
>  is leisure.
> High hangs a silver plate, reflecting blue hills.
>
> Long eyebrows of frozen green—how many
>  thousand years
> Pure and cool, indifferent to age—though a simurgh
>  in her mirror.
> Her autumn skin hardly feels the cold of a jade dress.
> The light of the void is fast and firm—water like sky.

This deserves some interpretation:

> The goddess has nothing to do but to finger her jewelry,
>  unchangeable metal like herself.
> Her headdress is a bird of metal, like the crown of a

medieval princess. (This line echoes the description of the headdress of Yang Kuei-fei as described in Po Chü-i's *Ch'ang hen ko:* "halcyon-blue tail cocked—a golden bird.")

Even palace gossip does not exist—everything was said eons ago.

A fairy reflector of metal shows the blue hills of mutable earth, here transformed into a static, impalpable scene.

The goddess herself is immortal—her green eye makeup needs no changing.

Unlike the vain simurgh who, watching its aging figure in a mirror (metal!) trembles with fear, the goddess, contemplating herself, is unmoved. (Simurgh is a Persian word naturalized in English. I use it as an equivalent of the fantastic Chinese *luan* — "phoenix" having been preempted for *feng*. I am pleased that Frodsham has adopted it in his translation of this poem.[22])

"Autumn" regularly connotes "white" and "cool"—and even "death," the changeless state. Her costume is not only jadelike in color and beauty, but is as rigid and cold as jade—and like ice and glass.

Her sky yields a fixed and unchanging light—it is the deep blue of the watery abyss.

There appears to be at least one important exception to Li Ho's seeming aversion to the common ninth-century practice of disguising courtesans, singing girls, mistresses, and court beauties as once popular goddesses who had fallen into neglect in upper-class religion. This is the poem titled "True Pearl—Belle of the Lo."[23] Inspecting the poem itself, it seems hard to avoid agreeing with the conclusion of Arai Ken, the Japanese Li Ho specialist, that this lovely pearl, like the moon maidens of Li Shang-yin, was an actual beauty of Lo-yang.[24] This decision is arrived at with some reluctance, in view of the fact that the great *T'u shu chi ch'eng* anthology lists the poem under the rubric of water goddesses. It begins with a pearl maiden flying down to Lo-yang out of the blue sky. She wears a bird-shaped crown, like the Lady of Cowrie Palace, and she dreams of her mountain in Szechwan, like the Wu shan goddess. She is a simurgh and a phoenix—indeed she has all of the attributes of a river fairy. But in the last four quatrains she is compared with the light ladies of Lo-yang—to their disadvantage. Is, then, a particular woman concealed here, or is Li Ho telling us that no mortal woman can compare with the divine creature of his linguistic epiphanies? In any case, his courtesan, if such she is, appears in supernatural guise. She is adorable—but strange and aloof, like a creature out of an ancient myth.

# 5 Dragon Women and Water Goddesses in Prose Tales

There be wise crocodiles whose daughters are more cunning than the witches of Lapland, and fairer than the Lotus of the Nile.

*Thomas Lovell Beddoes*
"Death's Jest Book," I, 1

## OLD-FASHIONED DRAGON WOMEN

By T'ang times the literary tradition of rainbow goddesses and dragon ladies had already been separated into two streams, one dominant in poetry, the other in prose. In brief the difference was this: since the production of the *Ch'u tz'u*, the poets had standardized—allowing for a variety of embellishments—the picture of a man, normally a king or young scholar replacing the archaic shaman, and his meeting with the goddess. She for her part appears in enchanting human form, close by her underwater home; she bears little resemblance to the scaly ondines of antiquity. The poet records their ecstasy and sad parting. The episode is transient. Sometimes the hero sees only a suggestion of the goddess in the mist, fragile and dreamlike, or hears only the echo of her song. Popular prose tales, on the other hand, and the oral tales that underlay them, had different emphases. They tended to take form around fully developed plots. The plot interweaves a series of episodes, some of them demanded by tradition, others the creation of the writer's fancy. They lead to various climaxes, some tender, some sad; some dramatic, some horrible; some polished, some coarse. Many of the themes developed in these stories have been studied in great detail, notably by W. Eberhard. I shall not try to recapitulate them here. Only a few that had particularly significant careers in the classical prose of the T'ang period will be mentioned. One of these themes, which has already often been alluded to, is that of the drowned girl who becomes a spirit of the water.[1] An early example is the tale of King Chao of Chou and the two maidens sent to him by the nation of Eastern Ou, presumably a non-Chinese people of the far southeast. This fable, which we have in its fourth-century (A.D.) form, does not come down to us as a fully developed short story, but it reveals a certain amount of crude characterization.[2] The girls were extremely beautiful and were talented musicians. They were so ethereal that they left no footprints, and they cast no shadows in broad daylight. The king took them boating in the Han-Kiang region, and there they all drowned. Temples were raised in their honor, and men prayed to them for protection from the dangerous dragons of the river. These nymphs are plainly akin to the goddess of the Hsiang River in her double form. Many of the features of poetry devoted to great female deities of the southern rivers—especially such traits as the evanescence of the divine women, their power of levitation, their superhuman loveliness, and their heavenly musicianship. On the other hand, the motif of the deified drowned woman, often a suicide, which lies at the heart of popular cult, is cmmonly absent from the more elegant upper-class variations on the old theme.

Occasionally a water sprite had the misfortune to be delivered helpless and hapless into the hands of an oaf:[3]

> Ch'en K'uei, a common person of Tan-t'u, built a fish-weir by the side of the Kiang. When the tide went out he found a woman six feet tall in the weir. She was well formed and complexioned, but lacked both outer dress and underskirt. With the departure of the water she was unable to move, and lay there in the sand. He spoke to her but she did not answer. A certain man came up and violated her. That night K'uei dreamed that she said, "I am the spirit of the Kiang. Yesterday I lost my way and fell into milord's weir, where a mean fellow abused me. Now I must explain to the Honored Spirit, who will kill him." K'uei did not presume to return home, and, with the coming of the tide, she went off by herself, following the water. Her violator subsequently fell ill and died.

This version of the great Kiang deity is still fairly close to the fish. Even more fishlike but much less sympathetic is a disguised nymph encountered in the central course of the river by the great essayist Liu Tsung-yüan when he was on his way into exile in the far south. This ninth-century tale[4] tells how, when the talented magnate was stopping at an inn, he was visited in three successive dreams by a woman dressed in yellow. She identifies herself as a resident of "Ch'u waters" and begs him to rescue her. The writer is unable to understand how he can save her life until, at a banquet given in his honor by a local official, he realizes that he is to have fish for dinner. He asks a flunkey about it, and is informed that a yellow-scaled fish had been netted the previous day. Its head has already been cut off, and it is ready to serve. Liu Tsung-yüan orders the fish thrown back into the Kiang. That night the woman appears in a final dream—headless. This short story, despite its horrible aspect, has been invested with an air of verisimilitude, and is rather far from being a simple folktale.

In the more elevated story world of true dragon women, "dragon" is an honorable epithet attached to a desirable feminine being. A good example appears in the obscure romance of Liu Tzu-hua. In this brief but elegant mystery, the heroine assumes the guise of a woman of the aristocracy and charms a magistrate out of his Ch'eng-tu office:[5]

One day about noon a calf-drawn carriage appeared unexpectedly. In front and behind, as escort and suite, were women on horseback. They came directly into the place of audience, and sent a messenger to announce to Liu, "The dragon woman will come to you now!" Shortly she descended from the carriage and, escorted by guards to left and right, went up the staircase and appeared before Tzu-hua. "Predetermined destiny," she said, "has joined me with milord as match and mate." So she stayed, and he ordered wine and music. After concluding the formalities with the utmost joy she departed. Thereafter their com-

ings and goings were customary, and everyone far and
near knew of them. Tzu-hua gave up his regular duties. It
is not known where he went, but the vulgar say that he
entered a dragon palace and finally attained the status of a
transcendent being of the water.

Except for the proclaimed dragon nature of the fair
charmer in this tale—she is brazen enough, in the classical Wu tradition—the plot resembles those of a hundred romances of the T'ang period that tell of fairy
women. The fox-fairy story is only the best known variation on the theme.

Dragon belles could even penetrate the imperial
palace. In Lo-yang, Hsüan Tsung had a daydream in
which a generously endowed young female appeared
to him, representing herself as the dragon woman responsible for the protection of the palace. Knowing
the sovereign's skill in music, she had come to ask for
the gift of a song to delight her kin, in repayment for
her constant vigilance. Still in a trance, Li Lung-chi (to
use his right name) invented a suitable tune and the
maiden disappeared. When he awoke he recreated the
dream song on his lute, and invited the court to the side
of the sacred pond—the home of the guardian lady—
for a performance. The goddess emerged, preceded by
a display of gushing and bubbling water. Li Lung-chi,
thrilled at the sight, had a temple erected by the side of
the pool, and ordered annual sacrifices to be offered to
her there.[6]

A rather special variation on the dragon woman tale
comes to us from the pen of the same Liu Tsung-yüan
whom we have just seen as the self-designated hero of
the story of the yellow fish. The unusual quality of this

second tale lies in the complete absence of sexuality, of ghostliness, or of fear. Instead it is marked by a spirit of humanity, coupled with a degree of scientific curiosity. It is titled "A Report on the Banishment of a Dragon."[7] A friend of the author named Ma Ju-tzu tells him that, at the age of about fifteen or sixteen years, he had been playing with some other youths. They saw a strange woman fall to the ground in a great blaze of light. She was cloaked in a crimson cape lined with white, and wore a trembling filigree crown. Outraged by the leering attentions of the young men, she announced indignantly that she was an independent spirit who had roamed freely among the stars, inhaling the essences of *yin* and *yang* while disdaining the inferior joys of P'eng-lai and K'un-lun, those earthbound paradises. But the gods, angered by her extravagance, had banished her to the world of men. Now her term of exile had only seven days to run, but she did not wish to spend even that short time contaminated by the filth of the town. Accordingly she retired into a Buddhist nunnery. At the allotted time she reversed her cape and whirled up into the sky in the form of a white dragon. Liu Tsung-yüan, trusting the veracity of his informant, expresses his regret at the unrefined treatment accorded this alien but elegant creature. His tale, sober yet incredible, belongs to a somewhat different class from that of the usual dragon-woman romance. It belongs properly to the genre of "banished transcendents" *(che hsien)* —stories of Taoist supermen and sylphine women consigned to a brief but usually not too tedious term amidst the contaminations of mundane life in punishment for some trespass unworthy of their exalted spiritual status. Even Li Po claimed to be such an earthbound martyr. Some females of the species, however, were not aloof to the blandishments of handsome young men—others protected their purity. The virginal indignation shown by Ma Ju-tzu's dragon lady, so unlike the majority of her sisters in this respect, is a case in point.[8]

Occasionally the theme of the dragon wife who takes a mortal lover or husband is given an exotic setting. Probably these are instances of travelers' tales brought to China by seafarers, camel drivers and the like, given a superficially Chinese color by common story-tellers, and finally picked up and transformed into refined prose by the important writers of classical wonder tales. Here is a short pseudoexotic romance of this kind, set in the oasis state of Khotan in Serindia:[9]

Southeast of the walled city of Khotan there is a great river which irrigates the fields of the entire nation. Suddenly its flow was interrupted. The king of that nation inquired about it of the monk Lo-hung, who said that it was the work of a dragon. The king then made offering to the dragon. From the midst of the water came a woman, skimming the waves. She saluted and said, "Your handmaiden's husband is dead. It is her wish to obtain a great vassal as husband. Then the water will be once more as of old." One of the great vassals begged leave to go, and the whole nation went to see him off. That vassal went into the water with carriage, rig, and white horse, but did not drown. After he had reached the middle of the river, the white horse floated out with a sandalwood drum and a manuscript in an envelope on its back. They took out the manuscript, which said, "Let the great drum be hung southeast of the city wall—should marauders come it will sound of itself." Afterwards, whenever raiders came, the drum did sound of itself.

Despite the predominantly Chinese character of its ingredients, this fictional courtship is surprisingly haunted by the sound of Drake's drum.

Earlier in this essay note was taken of post-Han examples of the birth of divine kings in consequence of the unions of male rainbow dragons and mortal women. Similarly, as Chinese society became increasingly male-oriented and even male-dominated through the post-Han centuries, mythology sometimes provided the nymphs of the rivers and lakes with husbands. These underwater kings were particularly evident in the north, the source of the tradition of male authority, while the meres and streams of the well-watered and somewhat un-Chinese Yangtze basin in the ancient southland allowed more freedom and independence to its fishy princesses. Even when later orthodoxy assigned them fathers, husbands, or brothers as their lords and protectors, these remained shadowy figures in literature, dim against the radiant vitality of the true rulers of the water—the lovely goddesses.

Eberhard has collected many examples of folktales which exemplify such common themes as fortunate young men rewarded for rescuing the son or daughter of a dragon king; the apparition of the daughters of dragon kings as lobsters, fish, and other inhabitants of the water; marriages of skillful musicians, ring bearers and other blessed youths to princesses in underwater palaces.[10] These folk motifs, in many variations, are also well known in short stories and novellas written in the literary language during the T'ang period. When, in such tales, a spectral maiden announces modestly that she is the daughter of a dragon king, she is simply identifying herself as a person of quality, well worth the attention of an educated and noble youth. Literary taste has taken over from folk art. The ancient and powerful Mistress of the River has not only become subservient to masculinity, but has become a sentimental dream girl, like the Undine of the romance by de la Motte-Fouqué.

Often there is more than an exalted exploration of passion by the lakeside on a warm June night. Sometimes the youthful hero achieves what the great kings and shamans of antiquity failed to do: he actually visits the goddess in her palace under the water. The dragon girls of these novellas appear to human males in human guise and in human surroundings, usually first on land. Usually terrestrial confinement is temporary punishment for some venial sin or domestic problem, analogous to the banishment of the airborne sylphs. The exile lasts until the hero, a successful but sometimes unwitting intermediary or catalyst, brings her back to her sub-aqueous home. These bold lads are latter-day substitutes for the entranced shamans of antiquity, whose souls courted the river goddesses on behalf of exalted human clients.

On the other hand, the dragon women sometimes appear in the *hsiao shuo* in true draconic form—but ordinarily only when in transit between their watery domain and the upper air. Then they may be thundering, roaring, and driving the black rain clouds. Such true daughters of dragon kings are usually clearly distinguished from the effete "literary" versions of the ancient water and rainbow women. The latter are dream women, lithe and lovely—but stripped of all taint of primitive cult. The two versions, draconic and delicate respectively, may even appear together in the same story. The *Lo shen chuan* will provide us with a notable example of such alter egos or doppelgängers. There the beautiful goddess of the river is an erotic idealization of a cultivated upperclass woman, although she derives ultimately from an ancient lamia. Her former shape and reptilian character are assumed by a knowledgeable but junior companion—a kind of herpetological but attractive young wiseacre. So it is also in other tales of dragon maids.

Before examining this particular case, let us look briefly at an example of a T'ang tale in which the true dragon woman is luckily freed from the conventional necessity of playing second fiddle to a glamorous spirit in human form—the star of the show. This story was included by Li Fu-yen in his series of wonder tales[11] written in the ninth century—an era notorious for skillfully contrived acounts of marvels—as a sequel to a similar set composed by the famous minister Niu Seng-ju.[12] Our example tells how a young vagabond named Liu Kuan-tz'u is befriended by a well-to-do man of Su-chou, who promises the vagabond a fortune if he will deliver a letter to the man's family in the north. The man—for such he seems—explains that he is from the Lo River region, and that the head of his household is a scaly creature who lives under a bridge. Liu Kuan-tz'u agrees, and on arriving at the bridge shuts his eyes and finds himself underwater. He is admitted to a rich mansion exactly like a well-appointed house in the world of men. Welcomed by the mother of his Su-chou friend, he delivers his message. Then, as he had been previously instructed, he asks to be introduced to the young daughter of the house. She reveals

herself as a lovely and sagacious young human female
of about sixteen years. (Shifting allusions to both the
anthropoid and the reptilian natures of dragons char-
acterize these stories, allowing the reader to indulge
his prejudices, whether they favor the fantastic or the
romantic. One may prefer, according to one's nature,
either bizarre metamorphoses or exotic damsels—or
both.) The daughter protects Liu Kuan-tz'u from her
voracious mother, whose dragon nature asserts itself
strongly when she seems on the point of making a meal
of the young man. But the wicked old woman gives the
youth a copper bowl to discharge the family's obliga-
tion. When he returns to the dry world, he sells this to a
foreigner for a huge sum of money. The stranger tells
him that this is the magic cup that protected the Kingdom of Kapiça. It had been stolen four years earlier by
the son of that very dragon family of Lo-yang. Therefore the dragon protector of Kapiça had reported the
theft to the gods (who are here superior to dragons),
and they in turn had designated Kuan-tz'u as its recov-
erer. So it would be possible for the thief—Liu's friend
in Su-chou—to resume his old life as a dragon with a
clear conscience.

A feature of this tale that slows the pace of the narrative somewhat is one that is quite characteristic of the
genre—the introduction of a disquisition on the physical and moral nature of dragons. In this one it takes
the form: "whatever one may suspect, dragons are
honorable in their dealings with men." One example:
when Liu Kuan-t'zu first arrives at the bridge of the
Lo, he reflects before knocking that he might perhaps
be acting unwisely. But he concludes that "a dragon

spirit would not dupe me!" Later, doubtful of the value of the copper bowl, he is heartened by the reflection that "dragon spirits are noble and trustworthy and would not dupe anyone."

KRAKEN WOMEN

The inherent nobility of dragonkind was not shared by the kraken subspecies—or, if a person put his faith in the nobility of krakens, there might be fatal consequences. The essential kraken nature is best illustrated in an old legend. King Chieh of the primordial Hsia dynasty kept a dragon woman in his palace. She was exceedingly lovely, and he called her "Kraken Concubine," even though she was a man-eater. Doubtless he took this risk because she had the power to prophesy good and evil days for him.[13] Few krakens of later times were so useful.

Krakens, male and female, often manifested themselves in the shape of a crocodile, alligator, or other fierce reptile. If a *lung* was a lord of the water, a *chiao* was a savage chief of the water—a pagan but powerful beast. In essence, however, the nature of a kraken, like that of a dragon, was female. The dictum of the T'ang poet Yüan Chen applied: an aged kraken turns into a weird woman or witchwife.[14]

The vengeful aspect of the kraken's character is illustrated in a short tale of the tenth century.[15] It tells how a man observed two krakens on the surface of a river and shot one of them. Later he was accosted in the market by a tearful woman clothed in white. She held an arrow, and cried out that his violent deed would be requited. On his way home the man suffered a violent death. But the ghost of any slaughtered beast would do as much. Indeed, not all kraken women were dangerous. A seventh-century tale, which develops as a rather ordinary fairy romance, tells of a young man enjoying a morning horseback ride in Loyang. He finds a beautiful girl weeping under a bridge of the Lo River. It transpires that she is the daughter of a kraken, banished from her home for some transgression of saurian ethics. The liaison proceeds in a conventional way and need not concern us further.[16]

But most krakens were positively malignant. In the following synopsis of a tenth-century wonder tale, a female kraken—no beauty—is a deadly lure.[17] A man sees a woman's body floating on the water. Supposing her to be a drowned person, he has his servant hook the corpse in to the shore. Suddenly it changes into a great snake and plunges back into the pool. When the man falls ill, a friend explains that old krakens, in the form of well-bedizened women, often roved the edge of this water, and the man realizes that the supposed dead woman was such a monster. A similar tale tells how several river women tried to lure a man into the water but were driven off by the villagers, who explained that they were actually krakens. Still another T'ang tale is set by a pool in a cave, but the lure is sexual—a siren's game:

A certain youth was passing by and saw a beautiful woman bathing in the water. She asked the youth whether he would play with her. Then she tugged and pulled the youth forward. So, removing his clothes, he went in—but then died by drowning. When his corpse floated forth after several days, it was a body that had completely dried up and withered away. The reason is surely that there was an old kraken lurking below in its den, whither it enticed men in order to drink their blood.[18]

Occasionally, however, even a *lung* female could prove to be as malignant as a *chiao*. It is told that a young man was traveling by boat in Kiangsi, and chanced upon a pleasant pavilion by a small lake. The building bore a placard: "Night-glowing Palace." There were a half dozen young women there, and they poured wine for him. One of them sang a sentimental song:

> The Sea Gate is joined to Tung-t'ing,
> But the sea is three thousand *li* away;
> Just once in ten years may I come back—
> Bitter anguish I suffer for Hsiao and Hsiang waters!

As the youth was leaving, he looked back from his boat and saw that the girls had disappeared. Subsequently he was informed that four persons had drowned at that very spot the previous night, but that another member of their party had escaped alive. The latter had stated that he had learned that the daughters of a dragon king of Lake Tung-t'ing were having a banquet there, and had taken the blood of the four men to use for wine. Remembering that he had accepted wine from these creatures, our horrified hero promptly vomited up several pints of blood.[19]

So it is with dragon women: sometimes ephemeral mistresses, sometimes authorities on dragon lore, sometimes bloodthirsty man-eaters. The archaic rain goddess had, by T'ang times, evolved into a number of distinct phyla, each with its interrelated genera and species, all infected and modified by medieval beliefs and attitudes and by new literary conventions. It can be said for all of the coquettish dragon daughters that, whether bloodthirsty or amiable, they were no weaklings. The same cannot be affirmed of the young men deluded by them: they take themselves too seriously, having no doubts about their own charm. They are bewildered, poor limp innocents, when the cold, lonely dawn comes. All of our authors take it for granted that a virtuous youth, well read in the classics as he may be, is no match for the wiles of a sultry lamia. We of the twentieth century may prefer a clever, picaresque hero, but the T'ang writers of fiction have never turned out such a marvel.

## SEA AND LAKE GODDESSES

Goddesses of large bodies of water, as distinct from river goddesses, do not appear early in Chinese literature, and when they do turn up they normally appear subjected to the authority of male divinities. A tale attributed to the third century A.D., but possibly later, tells how Wen Wang, one of the founders of the long defunct state of Chou, was visited in a dream by a beautiful lady who proclaimed herself the daughter of the god of T'ai-shan, which overlooks the eastern sea. She had been married off to the deity of the western sea.[20] This anecdote already sounds medieval; one would look in vain for something like it in authentic Chou literature. It has its counterpart—but without the device of an attribution to remote antiquity—in a story of the sixth century or later. This tale provides an early example of the theme of the young scholar seduced—or at least allured—by a water goddess. The setting is a waterway in Kiangsu late in the fifth century. A young man has moored his boat by a shrine, and he reposes there, watching the full moon. An outrageously lovely girl of sixteen or seventeen years appears to him. She is accompanied by a bevy of serving maids. She first tosses a tangerine into his bosom—a rather obvious invitation. They pass the night with wine and song and then she departs with her entourage. Next day he enters the shrine and finds her image painted on a wall along with those of her attendants. An inscription identifies her as "Maiden of the East Sea."[21] The apparition of a goddess near her temple is an ancient motif, and although in this case the lady is not closely identified with her native element, her sea was close at hand.

In time it became possible to imagine such a sea maiden, or her cousins, immersed in the oceanic waters themselves. So she became more dragonlike again, more truly a creature of the waves, more a mermaid than a princess. A characteristic tale of this later sort is one set in the tenth century, although the date of its writing is uncertain.[22] It tells of a young man who steals a pearl from the hat of an image of Chou Wu Ti that was kept in a monastery. He has many debts to redeem (a common theme in these stories) and happily manages to sell the gem to some foreigners for an immense sum. It is a magic pearl, and the westerners take him out to sea with them to observe a demonstration of its virtue. Various sea spirits appear and try to ransom the pearl. Finally, two beautiful dragon women appear, leap into the pot that holds the pearl, and merge with it to form an ointment. The strangers explain that these sprites are the protectresses of the pearl. Their leader then smears the ointment on his feet, walks out on the water, and disappears.[23] The usual amorous element, so dear to the hearts of the medieval Chinese, is absent from this tale, but the combination of indigent scholar, magic gem, and mysterious foreigner was extremely popular in T'ang times, and has sufficed to keep the female sea spirits away from the center of the stage.

An intermediate case is a tenth-century tale in which the goddess, attended by serving wenches—just as was the animated painting in our Kiangsu tale—is at one moment a very human person and at the next tinged with the animalian.[24] The narrator is an officer of the palace. He tells that once his ship encountered a severe storm at sea and was more than once in danger of sinking:

> The Sea Master said, "This is a deity of the sea in search of something. We must quickly cast the cargo of our ship into the water." When everything was gone a woman dressed in yellow, unmatched in the world for form and complexion, came to board the vessel. Four lackeys clothed in blue poled her boat: all had vermilion hair and boar's tusks—extremely fearsome of countenance. When at last she came up on the ship, she asked whether they had a fine wig of hair to give her. All of the men were flustered and frightened. They had no memory of such a thing, and could only say that everything had been given up. The woman said, "It is in a satchel on a wall at the rear of the ship." They found it there just as she had said. Up in a cabin of the vessel there was some jerky and salted meat. The woman took it to feed her four lackeys. It was observed that her hands were bird talons. She took the wig and departed, and the boat went on its way.

T'ang literature preserves a few accounts of foreign lake or sea goddesses (the language does not distinguish "large lake" from "sea"). All of them seem alien in origin but partly disguised by a thin Chinese veneer. Characteristically, two excellent examples have been preserved for us by that indefatigable collector of exotic lore, Tuan Ch'eng-shih. One tells of the progenitor of the Turks—a sea deity named Jama Shali.[25] Each day at sunset his daughter appears to him with a white deer and invites him into the sea, from which he emerges at dawn. A complicated folktale follows this prelude. It should be of some interest to future historians of ethnology,[26] but here we are beyond the realm of literature in the strict sense. Such is not so much the case with a seeming folktale which tells not of the north but of the west. Its setting is Tukharistan, confusingly governed by an ancient Persian king. This unlucky monarch wishes to build a new city, to be given a name which sounds suspiciously like "Bactria" (!). But the Sassanian (as he appears to be) does not do well with his building—his city walls simply will not stand. Only after his daughter cuts off her little finger and traces a line of blood around the circuit of the proposed walls will the masonry hold firm. She then turns into a lake goddess—the mistress of a clear pond, five hundred feet in circumference, outside the city.[27]

## THE ROMANCE OF THE SCHOLAR
## AND THE RIVER GODDESS

The place of the old river goddesses in T'ang fiction was a highly specialized one. Whether presenting them in exalted or debased condition, early medieval prose tended to show them more intimately than did poetry. In the poetic myths the hero (whether king, poet, or shaman—all, like Odin, are ultimately the same) meets a goddess in an ultimately unsatisfactory relationship on the banks of her river. She is indescribably beautiful but, even when helpful, aloof. In the newer prose tales, however, the hero (whether poet, young scholar, or magistrate—all ultimately the same in the mature Chinese tradition) chats intimately with her, and may even visit her in her pearly palace beneath the waves. She no longer flashes mysteriously out of rainbows and rain flurries like an elusive dragon but sways coquettishly in a diaphanous, rainbow-colored costume. Although she is only a dragon by courtesy, her mystery persists—and, like a dragon, her divine permutations are beyond mortal comprehension.

A glimpse of her subaqueous habitat is seldom afforded in the famous romances; we are allowed to assume that it is vaguely grand, rich and splendid. But a lesser tale of the ninth century which boasts no special supernatural heroine—although it is equipped with the customary well-educated hero—provides a good conventional view of the underwater palace. Our impoverished young scholar is revealed netting fish for his own supper in the Great Lake near the Yangtze estuary. He catches a magnificent specimen of a turtle and magnanimously liberates it. Years later the numinous reptile reappears alongside his boat and invites him to a banquet below, to which he is escorted by a respectful throng of turtles, fish, and alligators. He listens, as he takes his ease and pleasure in the lacustrine mansion, to the rich melodies sung by the deities of the Lake, the Kiang, and the Hsiang. These delightful singers, however, are not given any individuality in the story and need not concern us. The palace itself is provided with the usual furniture of the mansions of the elite on earth—fine pavilions, jeweled halls, colorfully woven dance carpets, and all the rest. These fine trappings are not just ready and waiting, they are magically produced for the occasion by the supernatural breath of attendant krakens and giant clams.[28] Excellent—but very unlike the shelly sitting rooms of antiquity.

## NÜ KUA

Such elegant surroundings were not the portion of all of the ancient goddesses, even the greatest, in the descriptions presented to T'ang readers. The fall of Nü Kua was the greatest of all. Seeming traces of her can be detected in anonymous snail girls in folktales and other simple stories.[29] An example is the odd account of Teng Yüan-tso of the ninth century who, says our story teller, had the good fortune to spend a night in a strange house with a lovely girl. In the morning he perceived that his love nest had been a snail shell, and that the delectable foods he had been served there had all been greenish slime.[30] Such a house seems just right for a spirit accustomed to a moist environment: naturally, wishing to ensorcel a young and attractive human, she added a rococo facing to her natural dwelling.

But it is futile to speculate how many altered fish and frogs might represent the old creator goddess. We know at least that the well-attested story of the disappearance of her barrow into the Yellow River points to the survival of her cult in some minimal fashion.

THE DIVINE WOMAN

Despite her continued high popularity in poetry, the destiny of the Divine Woman of Wu shan in T'ang prose was hardly better than that of Nü Kua. It would hardly be possible to count those stories that refer to her obliquely and in borrowed costumes; I have discovered two stories that are undeniably about her. In one of these, placed in the fifth century, a young aristocrat encounters a woman in fantastic costume. She smells of an unearthly perfume, and holds a flower. She takes him to a luxurious riverside palace, where he is given refreshment by a swarm of supernatural beauties. There is the customary wordy romance and the conventional early morning leave-taking. The youth discovers that he has passed the night in "The Shrine of the Divine Woman of Shamanka Mountain."[31] The motif of the illusory domicile remains constant in these little romances, although in this case the hero was spared the rather distasteful discovery that he had been housed with a mollusc. The usual scene is an old temple, a ruined mansion—a fox's den.

But even the Divine Woman could appear in as lowly a form as the latter-day Nü Kua. In prose she could be degraded to the condition of a fish—a lowly avatar of a dragon. An early medieval story tells that in the year A.D. 477 a man was angling in a stream. He caught a large white fish which promptly turned into a lovely maiden. He married her, and she left him only temporarily to visit her home at Kao-t'ang, the ancient cult site of the great rain and rainbow goddess.[32] She was the Divine Woman herself.

Another tale, set in the sixth century and perhaps

written in that period—certainly it was known in
T'ang times—tells of a rainbow woman who, although not specifically identified as such, is a plain and
patent version of the Wu shan maiden:

> In the Shou-yang Mountains a rainbow descended at eve-
> ning and drank at the source of a river. A woodcutter,
> Yang Wan, saw this from below the mountain pass. After
> a while it was transformed into a woman of sixteen or sev-
> enteen years. He marvelled at this, and questioned her.
> She did not speak. Accordingly he notified Yü-wen Hsien,
> the commander of the frontier garrison at Rush Ford, who
> had her seized, and made a report about it. Ming Ti [the
> reigning monarch of Wei] summoned her into his palace
> and saw that she was excellently beautiful of face and
> form. To his question she said, "I am the daughter of
> Heaven. I have come down among men for a brief
> period." The theocrat wished to force his favor on her, at
> which she showed extreme distress. He then ordered an
> attendant to press close and hold her tight. With a sound
> like a bell or stone chime she changed herself into a rain-
> bow and so ascended to the sky.[33]

And there we have it—no fetching allusions to blush-
ing cheeks, filmy chemises, or rich viands: only a
rather puritanical incarnation of a rainbow. Although
we may here be closer to the original legend in some
ways, this tale has done no great service to the history
of eroticism in China, otherwise so well served by the
mutations of the persona of the goddess in poetry.

THE LO DIVINITY

The Lo River goddess does much better in prose literature, chiefly because her story was already well known

from Ts'ao Chih's poem. At the end of the T'ang period, her tale was revived in a rather long and stylish prose piece with some real literary merit. It is one of a number of dragon tales written by Hsüeh Ying.[34] It embodies a faintly disguised commentary on Ts'ao Chih's work, and concludes with the common theme of T'ang novellas—a secular, romantic encounter between a young scholar and a beautiful spirit woman. The tale is at least as old as the ninth century, but it purports to tell of a much earlier period. In it, Hsiao K'uang, a private gentleman, playing his zither in quiet meditation near the Lo River one evening, attracts the attention of a mysterious woman. She identifies herself as the Lo Divinity and involves the young man in a critical discussion of Ts'ao Chih's famous composition. At one point she asks coyly whether Hsiao K'uang agrees with Ts'ao Chih's allusion to her as "as sinuous as a roving dragon." But this is the only reference made to her ultimate dragon nature. Otherwise she is at pains to show that she is the ghost of a real woman, that queen surnamed Chen, whose identity had been merged with that of the river deity Fu Fei by Ts'ao Chih, in order to avoid embarrassing and dangerous political implications. Once the historical background has been firmly established, and the "true" account of the divine lady's role in famous events of the past carefully set forth, the narrative can proceed. A maid servant appears and announces, "The Silk Weaving Maiden has now arrived!" Here we are introduced to the most interesting personage in the tale, despite the nominal priority of the goddess of the Lo. The dragon nature of the Silk Weaver is much closer to the surface, but she is also something of a professor and scholiast.

Indeed both of these divine women are more high toned and didactic than are their radiant counterparts in most T'ang novellas. The goddess describes the newcomer as "the dear daughter of the dragon lord of the Reach of the Lo." Now begins a catechism, with Hsiao K'uang as catechumen. The responses of Silk Weaver contain sly attacks on the writings of other T'ang scholars, blandly treating their fiction as alleged fact. A notable example is the story of Liu I—clearly already widely circulated—which we shall examine closely later. There is also a certain amount of lore of the wiseacre sort—especially "Five Elements" doctrine—grafted onto the dialogue. Silk Weaver explains well-known historical and supernatural events in what seem to her to be "rational" terms. She takes special pride in debunking common hypotheses about the nature of dragons. Let us take up the story at this point:

> K'uang accordingly spoke to Silk Weaver saying, "In the world of men in recent days a certain person told of the spirit marriage of Liu I. Was there such an occurrence?" "Just four or five parts of it in ten can be accepted," said the woman, "The rest is all ornamentation. You must not be deluded!" K'uang said, "I heard somewhere that dragons dread iron. Is that so?" "A dragon is a mutation of spirit," said the woman. "Iron, stone, gold, jade—whatever it may be—are all readily permeable to it. Why should it stand in particular awe of iron? What it fears are krakens and hydras and their ilk." Next K'uang said, "The son of the Lei clansman[35] had girded on the sabres of Feng City when he came to the Ford of Yen-p'ing. They leaped into the water and were transformed into dragons.[36] Is that so?" The woman said, "A fable indeed! Dragons are akin to Wood,[37] while a sabre is Metal. Since Metal overpowers Wood, the former does not generate

the latter. How could such an alteration or transformation be possible? Surely it is not the same as a sparrow going into the water to become a clam,[38] or a pheasant going into the water to become a clam monster![39] But a treasure sword is a numinous object. It is Water that Metal generates, and so it went into the water. Master Lei would simply not have been able to plunge into the spring by himself. When later he searched for his sword and did not find it, he said falsely that it had become a dragon. Moreover, Lei Huan said only that it was transformed and gone, while Chang Szu-k'ung[40] merely said that the two had achieved final union. Neither of them claimed that they became dragons. Even allowing that the swords were numinous and unusual, still they were beaten, cast, forged, and refined by human beings—they were not spontaneous objects. Knowing this, it is clear that they could not have become dragons." K'uang then said, "What about the case of the shuttle that was transformed into a dragon." "A shuttle is wooden," she said. "Basically dragons are of the Wood category. What, after all, is astonishing in the alteration or mutation of something so that it returns to its base?" Then K'uang said, "The alterations and mutations of a dragon are like those of a spirit. Why then, when one was ill, was Ma-shih Huang sent for to heal it?"[41] The woman said, "Doctor Huang was an Exalted True One from the Upper Realm. He felt compassion for horses, which take burdens on their backs and carry them afar. Therefore he became a physician for horses. High Heaven sent down a speculum and transformed it into a disease between the corners of the dragon's lips, wishing to test the ability of Doctor Huang. Afterwards the dragon ascended to Heaven carrying him upon its back. Heaven had simulated it—it was not that the dragon truly had a disease." K'uang then said, "Is there such a thing as a dragon's craving for the blood of swallows?" "Dragons are pure and insubstantial," said the woman. "Their food and drink is the dewy vapor of night. If they were to eat swallow's blood how could they either take action or conceal themselves? Such cravings are doubtless limited to the likes of krakens and clam monsters. Have no faith in fabrications and fictions! All of this is the extravagant and baseless verbiage of the Four Lords of the Liang Levee, nothing more!" Then K'uang said, "What does a dragon enjoy?" "It enjoys sleep," she said, "if large—a thousand years; small ones—not less than several hundred years. They lie supine in their grottoes and holes, and accumulate a burden of sand and silt between the scales of their armor. Sometimes a bird will bring the seed of a tree in its beak and let it go on top of one. Then the armor will crack open and give birth to a tree. Only when it is entirely enfolded does the dragon awake and become aware of this. Then it shakes itself and quickly refines its activity. Shedding its corporeal frame, it enters into vacuity and nullity. Clarifying its spirit, it returns to the silence of extinction.[42]

> Form and vitality alike, of spontaneous origin,
> Adapted to the functions of mutability,
> Are dispersed into the true void.
> While not integrated into an embryo,
> While not congealed and crystallized,
> It is like a creature settled in the formless,
> Elemental and rarified in undifferentiated tenebrosity!

At this point in time, even with its hundred skeletal segments and its five corporeal frames, it can put itself entirely inside a mustard seed. Whether it is in action or in repose, there is no place it cannot go. It has the natural art of returning to the primordial and retiring into the rudimentary, and thus vies in its achievements with the Fashioner of Mutations." K'uang then said, "To refine one's activity as a dragon does—through what gateway is that acquired?" "How is it different," said the woman, "from an

Exalted True One's art of refinement? If a superior gentleman refines them, his form and spirit progress together. If a middling gentleman refines them, his spirit leaps up while his form sinks down. If an inferior gentleman refines them, his form and spirit fall together. Also, when the time for refinement is at hand, the vital breath is brisk while the spirit is clogged. There is a creature that emerges from this, as Lao tzu says: 'All indistinct and formless—in its midst there is a creature.' As to its relation to the Occult and Imperceptible, I dare not let that leak out or expose it, fearing lest Highest Heaven denounce and ostracize me."

Having thus rebuked her inquisitor for inquiring about matters beyond his comprehension, Silk Weaver turns to the refreshments—wine, and animated but not didactic conversation. Young K'uang is seated, as our author puts it, between "a rose gem branch to his left and a white jade tree to his right." Intimacy increases and we are given delicate hints of lovemaking. At cockcrow, the hero is obliged to leave his two dragon ladies. Each of them composes a poem to commemorate the sad moment. Silk Weaver's quatrain goes like this:

> Weaving silk at the bottom of a spring: few joys
> or amusements:
> Now instead I urge Master Hsiao to drink up
> this beaker!
> Sad to see the jade zither plucked for a parting crane—
> But take a limpid tear, a drop of true pearl!

Hsiao K'uang himself is, of course, the parting crane to whom the stirrup cup is offered. Tear and pearl are identical: it is the solidified tear of a mermaid, a weaver of shark silk—that is, of the *pinikon* made from the byssus of mussels. So her verses foreshadow the actual parting gift: the Lo Goddess offers K'uang a shining pearl along with a feather of a halcyon kingfisher—symbol of the blue sky. (Both presents had been mentioned long ago in a ritual exchange of gifts described in Ts'ao Chih's *Lo shen fu*.) The junior dragon girl also gives him a length of her *pinikon,* saying, "If a man of western origin offers to buy this, you should not let it go for less than a myriad metal coins." Finally, after prophesying immortality for the youth, the goddesses vanish. Hsiao K'uang went on to Sung, the sacred mountain, and there related his adventures to a friend. So they came to be written down. But afterwards he left this world, presumably for divine delights.

Our author has done an ingenious job with his double pastiche, based on the work of Ts'ao Chih in the first instance and on the Nine Songs and Sung Yü in the second. Most of the popular T'ang themes are present, neatly interwoven: the romance between an educated youth and a supernatural maiden; the heavy patina of magic and popular Taoism, grafted onto conventional "Confucian" clichés; the compendium of dragon-lore rationalized in terms of standard, upper-class, metaphysical belief; the enriching gift eagerly sought by a mysterious foreigner; the euhemerization of mythical characters, and all the rest of it—some from vulgar lore, some from the conventional religion of the elite. Hsiao K'uang, the ostensible hero, however, is never well characterized, while the Lo Divinity, in the form of a prettified princess, seems merely to simper. Silk Weaver, despite—or perhaps because of—her solemn pretensions as an expert on her own race, comes off best. Although she accepts advanced, even radical, views about the ontology of dragons—views unknown to the dragon masters of antiquity—she strikes us as would an attractive and somewhat mysterious visitor from another planet, in her first year of graduate studies at an earthly university, mightily anxious to subdue her girlishness while magnifying her newly acquired intellectual sophistication.

## THE HSIANG CONSORT

Reduced to the condition of an indignant court lady, determined to keep her identity distinct from that of a venerable river spirit, the Lo Goddess enjoyed a brief but pleasant resurrection by way of the writing brush of Hsüeh Ying. Otherwise she was neglected by T'ang prose writers—or so it seems from the evidence of the extant literature. The goddess (or, for many, the goddesses) of the Hsiang fared rather better, having been granted almost as much attention and admiration in the classical short story of that period as she had been in poetry. All in all, among educated men at any rate, she appears to have been the most vital of the old water and fertility goddesses who survived into the early medieval period.

The double goddess had appeared in prose centuries before, in a "biographical" tale about "The Two Consorts of the Kiang," who are plainly identical with the consorts of the Hsiang.[43] This fictitious Taoist hagiography shows two divine women in human guise roaming the banks of the Kiang and Han rivers. They meet a man and engage him in an amusing word game with erotic overtones. They disappear without his having understood that they were goddesses. The whole

makes little more than a brief and inconclusive anecdote.[44] A somewhat different version of the same story
tells of a man strolling by the Han.[45] There he "saw
two women, both of them gorgeously costumed and
splendidly made up; they carried with them a pair of
luminous pearls as large as chickens' eggs." This sen-
tence, absent from the received version of the text,
provides the ladies with magical night-shining gems.
These are the regular playthings of dragons, and show
symbolically that the strange women are water spirits
and cryptodragons.[46]

The twin goddesses do not appear as simply as this
in most T'ang short stories—indeed, they lend themselves to a variety of treatments, sometimes in rather
unexpected ways. Occasionally they were subjected to
lewd and insulting treatment. Here is a ninth-century
example:

> There is a temple to Shun at Rush Ford, and also temples
> to Fairy Radiance and Maiden Bloom at the side of Shun's
> temple. The aspect of their earthen images shows quite
> perfect skill and rich beauty. During "opened Perfection"
> [A.D. 836-841][47] Lu Szu-tsung of Fan-yang was vacation-
> ing from his duties at Rush Ford. One day, as he strolled
> by Shun's temple with a number of friends, he came to the
> temples of Fairy Radiance and Maiden Bloom. Szu-tsung
> said in jest, "I should like to become the client of these
> children of God—is it permissible?" and making the dou-
> ble bow he invoked them for some time. The members of
> the party all addressed him, saying "Why these offensive
> and cheap words? They will outrage the deities!" Szu-
> tsung laughed, and became more and more drunk. After
> this he walked alone many times to the Temple of Fairy
> Radiance, and got drunk on wine there and made many

indecent and outrageous remarks. But shortly after this he was taken ill, and had to be carried home on a shoulder litter. He appeared to be trembling in agitation—the sweat draining out of his body. That evening he passed away. His house boys saw more than ten persons seize Szu-tsung and drag him out through the gate, going off toward the Temple of Shun. When they looked at Szu-tsung, there were very many red lines on his back, as if he had been flogged. All of the people of Rush Ford marvelled at this incident.[48]

We have already set forth the story of the attempted rape of a rainbow goddess at Rush Ford. Apparently we have here another case of the fusion of the Divine Woman with the Hsiang Consort. In any case, the goddesses were not mocked with impunity, and their husband Shun was quick to punish a base human rival.

Other men had more fortunate encounters with Shun and his wives. Here is another T'ang tale:

The favorite younger brother of Hsiao Fu was in his youth devoted to the Way, and did not go into public service. His medicine and food were polypores and cinnamon. He was skilled at the zither, and excelled particularly in the Airs of the South. So he journeyed in Heng and Hsiang. There he tied his boat to the bank of the Kiang. He saw an old man carrying books on his back and holding a zither. Young Hsiao bowed, sat down and said, "You must play the zither well, father—have you achieved the Airs of the South?" "I have long done them well," he said. So he begged him to strum one, and it was wonderful beyond measure. Afterward he had all of his art passed on to him. They drank several goblets of wine. When he asked him where he lived, [the old man] smiled and did not reply. When he [Hsiao] returned northward and came to the mouths of the Yüan and Kiang, he ascended the bank to polish his Airs of the South. There was a young girl with double topknots, holding a small bamboo basket in her hand. She said, "The Ladies are close by. They are fond of the zither, and I wish to hurry off and report to them." "Why did you come here" asked Hsiao. "Only to gather fruit," she said. Just as she was leaving she turned again and said, "The Ladies will summon your lordship!" Hsiao remained in his boat a long time. Then he thought of taking a leisurely walk, but before long a painted barge came, with a gray-head at the oars. Hsiao climbed into it. They proceeded more than a mile and found a gateway and guesthouses, very splendid. The youth was summoned up into the hall, and there he saw two beautiful persons. He bowed before them, and one beauty said, "You should not be astonished that we welcome you. We are aware, lord, that you are skilled in the Airs of the South. We too have long loved them. But it has been long since we polished or practised them, so that we have forgotten half of them. We should like to have you pass them on to us." The youth therefore performed them for them. The beauties also commanded him to take up the zither. When Hsiao had finished plucking it, the two beauties and their attendants hid their faces and wept. They asked the youth from what person he had learned them, so he told them of the old gentleman, describing his appearance in detail. The beauties shed tears and said, "It was Shun! This too shows that the High God sent this young lord to receive them and transmit them to us! We are the two consorts of Shun. Shun has become Supervisor of Disciples in the Ninth Heaven. We have now been separated for a thousand years. The years are many since we learned this song, and we had forgotten it." They then kept the youth to sip a few cups of tea. As he was announcing his departure the youth said, "Although I prize your generosity and esteem your benevolence, I would prefer not to mention this to other men." Then he went out the gate, boarded the painted barge again, and returned to the place where he had been plucking the zither. The next day he went back to look for them, but there was nothing there any more to be seen.[49]

This rather pleasant, well-integrated, but unassuming variant on the familiar theme of the encounter of a young scholar with a divine woman follows the usual pattern, but lacks the common ingredient of amorous repartee — to say nothing of a colloquium on supernatural zoology of the kind that was so prominent, for instance, in the story of the Lo Divinity. However, the author has stressed such points as the special diet of his hero, implying that he is a searcher for means to join the ranks of the immortals. Skill at the zither was a refined and classical art, suitable to a person of sensibility with a feeling for fine old things. We have remarked before on the attempts of several T'ang scholars to find contemporary analogues of the "Songs of the South" in the folk music and songs of the southlands: young Hsiao is the fictional embodiment of all such romantic musicologists. Shun does not appear as a glorious deity here. He has become a venerable sage — or so he appears on earth when he is on leave from his dignified magistracy in the sky. The luxurious but evanescent palace is typical, as is the theme of an earthly go-between by spirits. In short, we have a rather good example of a T'ang supernatural story, in which popular motifs have been carefully selected and blended. It is told in a plain, straightforward manner, without the common embellishments of extended descriptions of rich furniture or sequences of sentimental poems. But the goddessess, despite the divinity they claim, have been reduced to a pair of rich widows, trying to remember the musical soirees they once enjoyed with their eminent husband, who is now engaged in more important activities elsewhere.

A very different kind of story involves the poet Li Ch'ün-yü, who loved the central lakes and rivers—and their spirits as well. It is said that when he retired from public office and was on his way homeward, he stopped at the Shrine of the Two Consorts at Yellow Tumulus. There he left a series of verses dedicated to them. The poems remark on the wild condition of the temple grounds, the defaced old stone inscription, the sad cries of the hawk cuckoo at sunset (symbol of a dead king) and the long distance that separates the shrine and its divine inhabitants from the place of Shun's death. While Li was polishing up one of these stanzas, he was visited by apparitions of Fairy Radiance and Maiden Bloom, who promised him "an excursion with clouds and rain" two years later. Then they vanished. Li gave due honor to their images, and continued on his way. Later he met his old boon companion Tuan Ch'eng-shih, the collector of cultural and linguistic curiosa and at that time a county official in Kiangsi, and told him about the curious affair at the shrine. Tuan made a jest about the mysterious encounter: the mention of an affair of "clouds and rain" obviously held out the prospect of lovemaking with the two divine women two years hence. "I had no idea that you would make a cuckold of Shun," he said. But two years later Li Ch'ün-yü died in Hung-chou. The rendezvous was to be in the world of ghosts.[50] There appears to be an element of fact in this melancholy

tale, but it is hard to separate it from the fiction, as so
often is the case with stories about prominent T'ang
personages when those stories were written by their
contemporaries or near contemporaries. Even the vision of the goddesses at their famous temple need not
be invention. The real possibility of such occurrences
was firmly impressed on the medieval Chinese mind.

The draconic element shows forth rather more
prominently in a version of the Hsiang goddess in a
well-known tale written early in the ninth century by
Shen Ya-chih. Shen Ya-chih was a leader and innovator in the *ch'uan ch'i* movement. This means that
his example was influential in popularizing fantastic
stories written in good but not over-ornamented classical Chinese. The author writes that he heard this tale
told in 818, but it is clearly a work of art of his own
devising based on a familiar theme.[51] In a brief preface
he characterizes the story as an affair of "uncanny
glamour," familiar to many depraved persons although poorly understood by them. His purpose is to
give a proper interpretation of it to literary men who
might appreciate it on an elevated level. The tale opens
in Lo-yang and links a lovely heroine automatically
with the goddess of the Lo River, although eventually
a connection with the more exotic goddesses of the
Hsiang River appears too. The divine creature is very
much a secular belle. She is discovered weeping under
a bridge in the moonlit dawn. The male protagonist,
named Cheng, is a scholar employed at the palace
school in Lo-yang—it is the reign of the Empress
Wu—and he is on his way to his place of employment.
The beautiful girl claims to be an orphan, mistreated
by her brother's wife. Therefore she has decided to

drown herself. Young Cheng persuades her to go home with him, and he names her Far Floater because of her familiarity with the *Ch'u tz'u* and because of the incomparable verses that she knew how to set to the traditional tunes. An extended example named "Verses to the Light and the Wind" is given. It is in the conventional *fu* style and alludes mysteriously to her aristocratic condition in former times. Because Cheng is not very well off, from time to time the maiden produces a piece of fine silk which they sell to foreign merchants for a large sum. After several years, when the scholar is about to leave for Ch'ang-an, the girl confesses that she is a junior daughter in the palace of a kraken of the Hsiang River, banished to the sublunary world. Her term of exile has now expired and she must say farewell to her lover. His protests are in vain. Ten years later, Cheng's brother holds a great party in a building overlooking the holy isle in Lake Tung-t'ing, and young Cheng improvises a sad couplet plainly linking his lost love with the great goddess of the Hsiang River. He has hardly finished when a gorgeously decorated boat comes up, carrying a godlike company and divine musicians. Among them is a woman resembling Far Floater. She performs a dance, while singing sadly of the impossibility of reunion. Then the whole apparition disappears in a sudden squall of rain.[52]

Many familiar motifs appear here, among them the exiled goddess penalized with a fixed term in a lowly condition among men; reminiscences of the *Ch'u tz'u;* the gift of a costly dragon silk, so much desired by rich westerners (the reader will recall that both of these two last themes were prominent in the *Lo shen chuan;*

there are also strong resemblances between Silk
Weaver and Far Floater); the interspersed sentimental
poems; the final epiphany in clouds and rain; the ultimate identity of dragon, river goddess, dream image,
and lost love.

The most melodramatic example—and also perhaps the most sophisticated—of a T'ang novella about
a dragon woman is the story of Liu I, written by Li
Ch'ao-wei in the eighth century.[53] There is an easily
accessible translation of this story available. What follows here, therefore, is only a brief synopsis.

Liu I, failed candidate, is returning to his home on
the Hsiang River when he encounters a sad but beautiful woman tending goats by the roadside. She identifies herself as the youngest daughter of the Dragon
Lord of Tung-t'ing. She has fled the home of her husband, a wastrel. She asks Liu I to deliver a message to
her parents as he journeys southward. He undertakes
the assignment—and there is a suggestion that the two
might meet again. Liu I goes on to the lake, where he
finds the Dragon Lord in his splendid palace. He ac-
knowledges that he is human, but a fellow native of the
Hsiang region, and delivers the letter. There is loud
lamentation throughout the palace. A great red male
dragon makes a spectacular exit to avenge the family
honor: "A thousand thunders, a myriad lightning bolts
shot around its body, while graupel, snow, rain, and
hail all fell at once." Soon the dragon returns with
the lost daughter, and the occasion is celebrated with
feasting and music. Because the red dragon has mean-
while eaten her obnoxious and inconvenient husband,
the girl is made available to Liu I, but he declines the
honor. Returning to the upper world as a rich man, he

weds twice, but both marriages end in the death of his spouse. He marries a third time, and discovers that his new wife is a human avatar of the dragon lord's daughter. She grants him ten thousand years of life with her. After twenty years together they both leave the world of men and take up residence in Lake Tung-t'ing as Taoist immortals.

Although the plot of this story is not original, it is richly ornamented and contains enlightening information about the illusory forms assumed by divine beings when they appear to men. For instance, when Liu I inquires about the goats of the dragon king's daughter, she explains that they are "rain builders" and "akin to thunderclaps." There is an echo of Silk Weaver's textbook wisdom here. Again, inside the palace the dragon lord discusses the "Fire Canon" with a venerable Taoist adept. This book expounds the nature of men, who have an affinity with the element Fire, just as dragons have power over Water. As normally, the submerged palace is in all respects more like a rich mansion on earth than an archaic lake god's shell-studded house. Moreover, except for the avenging red dragon as he goes on his way to rescue the maiden, all of these divine beings appear to Liu as handsomely garbed human beings. They hold very earthly conversations, and their songs and entertainments could have taken place in the T'ang capital. Indeed the dragon girl, describing her father's palace, says "There is no discernible difference between Tung-t'ing and the capital city." In short, the old gods have, as usual, been transformed into the actors in a human drama. Even the great Hsiang Goddess is the helpless daughter of a mighty king. Only a few conventional clichés, like paper wings on a schoolboy angel in a Christmas play, hint at their reptilian nature and their full adaptation to life in the water.

# 6 Conclusion

This inquiry has sought to disclose something of the entanglement of myth, religion, symbolism, and romantic imagination in a segment of T'ang literature. It is evident that even the subtlest poem or the smoothest tale confuses myth with history, legend with fact, pious hope with rational belief. In so doing, it expresses commonly held opinions about the ancient and supernatural worlds.

The writers of T'ang liked to present goddesses as etherealized human beings. They tried to illuminate their natures and activities with fine words, but sometimes the handsome figures of speech they employed served better to illustrate supposedly eternal truths — components of established morals and metaphysics — than to make original and attractive poetic configurations.

Still, from the kaleidoscope of literature, a fairly consistent image emerges. Most T'ang writers thought of the nature goddesses as the glorified spirits of ladies long since dead who had seized, legitimately or not, particular lakes and rivers as their private domains, and so were able to have important effects on the lives of men. As the literary men of T'ang made their interminable journeys toward new country posts, or into exile, or on recreational excursions, they prayed to these transformed divinities. But they were not addressing eternal natural spirits at all—their prayers aimed to move ghostly survivals, supernatural relics of prominent persons of the past who had the good fortune to be immortalized in classical literature. The Lo River goddess was typically thought of as the earthbound soul of a dead queen. The goddesses of the Hsiang River were the corporeal spirits of two lovely widows whose good luck it had been to have gained the affection of a great prehistoric king. Nü Kua had once ruled over all men, it was thought, just as did the Empress Wu later. Mythology had become history.

This transformation is particularly marked in the T'ang prose tales. For example, the story of Liu I presents a divine woman who resembles closely the kind of woman most admired by cultivated persons in medieval China. Even when dragon women, plainly labeled as such, appear in these stories, they are more protean nymphs than holy reptiles, and they normally reveal themselves to men in human shape.

In poetry, on the other hand, the ogling courtesan at one extreme and the lovely dragon girl at the other, both so conspicuous in the prose tales, are usually replaced by tantalizing visions of supernatural loveliness, little tainted with the specifics of the boudoir or of reptilian prehistory.

In both media, the water goddesses, however glossed they may be with gauze and rouge, however remote they seem from their fierce and powerful originals, however much—in short—they may resemble tinted photographs or fashionably painted dolls, remain pitiless nature spirits and lethal sirens underneath. Whether they are represented as female crocodilians or as nightclubbing naiads, ultimately they see their lovers as their natural prey, to be drained either of blood or of virility. Only occasionally, when tinctured with the lore of popular Taoism, do they hold out the prospect of something like lasting bliss—but these philosophical ladies are truly dominos in a masquerade, by no means the water spirits and dragon women whose wardrobes they have plundered.

Nevertheless the prose tales seem more innocent— closer to unsophisticated taste—than do the poems, and the young heroes who inhabit them resemble the archetypal shaman more than do the male personae projected by the poets into their idealized visions of the elusive goddess.

Both genres present the faded images of an ancient hero, appropriately modified by medieval taste and trappings. The prose writer sends his young Gilgamesh on a hazardous journey whose modern setting barely conceals the underlying classical legend, and the dazzled youth follows his coy new beloved under the waves entirely in the manner of the ancient and universal "quest" myth.[1] The poet, on the other hand, yearns and dreams—and paints himself and his strange visions into his word pictures.

# Notes

INTRODUCTION

1   Hawkes (1967), 72.
2   Hawkes (1962).
3   Davidson (1968), 118.
4   E. G. Pulleyblank, with persuasive evidence, believes the name to be an originally non-Chinese word for "river," surviving from a time before the Chinese successfully controlled the watershed of the Kiang. The name is presumably cognate to Cham *kraung*, Mon *krung*, and other words.


CHAPTER 1

1   Darwin (1795), 535.
2   TCTC, 239, 4a.
3   Hastings (1962), XII, 717.
4   Darwin (1795), 130.
5   Schafer (1956), 73.
6   See Eberhard (1968), 43 and 205, for the chain of connections, and for the celebrations of the third day of the third month that were the special prerogatives of water goddesses.
7   Schafer (1963b), 80, 243; Schafer (1967b), 160. For the Shakespearean phrase, see "A Midsummer Night's Dream," Act II, Scene 1.
8   KY, Ch'u yü, b, 203. "Shaman" here translates *hsi,*

"shamanka" translates *wu*. The whole passage is translated in Thiel (1968), 152. Thiel's article is a very important study of early Chinese shamanism.

9    Sierksma (1966), 71. See also, inevitably, Eliade (1964), *passim*.

10   YYTT, *hsü chi*, 2, 187; Groot (1907), 1227-1228, notes another T'ang story of a woman surnamed Hsüeh who served or coerced this spirit.

11   Sierksma (1966), 73.

12   See Schafer (1951), 154-156 and *passim*.

13   TS, 48, 6a.

14   ChTS, 89, 2a; TS, 115, 1b.

15   *P'u wu yü jih*. Schafer (1951), 136.

16   CS, 94, 1325b; this passage is translated in Waley (1956), 11.

17   So they appear in *The Anglo-Saxon Chronicle* for the year A.D. 793. See Plummer and Earl (1965), 55.

19   *Beowulf*, xxxii, 2272-2274. My translation.

19   Hastings (1962), I, 513.

20   Marianne Moore, "The Plumet Basilisk."

21   Hastings (1962), XI, 408, 412-415.

22   This was in 714. Rotours (1966), 263-265; Eberhard (1968), 239.

23   Other cognate binoms may be found in *Tz'u t'ung*, I, 25-26.

24   Coral-Rémusat (1936), *passim*.

25   Thomas (1959), 147.

26   Mori (1969), 220. The *\*ghung* was sometimes a white halo around the sun, especially when styled "white rainbow" *(po hung)*.

27   SWCT, ch. 11 "lung."

28   Hastings (1962), 712-713.

29   Wen (1961), 53-57.

30   TS, 36, 11a.

31   PWC, quoted in *Kan ying ching*, quoted in turn in TPKC, 464, 1b.

32 Usually a rain summoner, the freshwater alligator of China was sometimes regarded as a harbinger of war because of his armored hide. See, for instance, TS, 34, 5a.

33 P'i Jih-hsiu, "Yung hsieh," CTS, 615, 7099.

34 Li Ch'ün-yü, "Fang yü," CTS, 570, 6605.

35 CS, 36, 1184d.

36 CS, 97, 1337b.

37 PPT, "Lun hsien."

38 TaCTC, in TPKC, 418, 1b.

39 TS, 36, 10a.

40 Schafer (1954), 107-108.

41 Wen (1935), 850, citing Mao's commentary on the "Odes," and IC respectively.

42 LH, 1, 84 "Lung hsü."

43 Schafer (1967b), 220, has further information.

44 TS, 186, 3b-4a.

45 Schafer (1963b), 109.

46 Schafer (1963b), 109; Schafer (1967b), 85, 220-221.

47 SIC, a, 3a.

48 Li Ho, "Ch'in wang yin chiu," LCCKS, 1, 56-58. Many editions of Li Ho's poems are readily available and have been consulted for this study. Bibliographic references will be uniformly to LCCKS, one of the Li Ho collections incorporated in Yang (1964).

49 TFSPC, quoted in PTKM, 43, 22a. This text may be the same as the *Tung-fang Shuo chuan* attributed to Kuo Hsien of the Han period, which has been excerpted in many *hsiao shuo* collections.

50 TS, 36, 10b.

51 TS, 36, 10b.

52 TS, 36, 10a. This reign is little noticed in our standard tables of dynasties. The youth assumed the era name *T'ang lung* "Eminence of T'ang." He died in 714 at the age of seventeen and is known posthumously as Shang Ti.

53 TS, 36, 10b.

54   SC, 4, 0051c; Schafer (1951), 149.
55   Eberhard (1937), 102-104.
56   See many examples in Eberhard (1968), 39-40, 231-233.
57   Schafer (1967b), 219.
58   SC, 1, 0006a.
59   WS, 1, 1903c.
60   WS, 8, 1921d. E. G. Pulleyblank, in a speech to the CIC
     Institute at the University of Minnesota on July 1, 1970,
     gave many examples of these solar visitations during the
     Six Dynasties period.
61   Hastings (1962), XI, 409.
62   ChTS, 2, 1a.
63   Hastings (1962), XII, 708.
64   Hawkes (1967), 80.
65   Wen (1960), 143-148.
66   Wen (1960), 153-154, citing *Han fei tzu, Yen tzu ch'un
     ch'iu,* and *Sou shen chi.*
67   Schafer (1967a), 58.
68   Hersholt (1942), 57. From "The Little Mermaid."
69   Hastings (1962), XI, 418, supplies the well-known facts.
70   Wen (1960), 155-156 points out that in later texts the
     god takes a divine rather than a human wife, and some-
     times even gives his own daughter to a human being.
71   Darwin (1795), 118.
72   TC, Hsiang, 21.
73   Several instances in TPKC, 464-472.
74   Schafer (1963c), 91.
75   Graves (1958), 232, n.4; Hastings (1962), IV, 592.
76   HHHP, 4, 128. The same painter also did "Picture of the
     Dream of Ch'u Hsiang Wang about the Divine Wom-
     an." This catalogue does not list a single goddess paint-
     ing surviving from the T'ang.
77   Needham (1954), 163.
78   Hastings (1962), XI, 407, 410.
79   Glueck (1965), 359-360, 381-382, 391-392.
80   Eberhard (1968), 242, citing Creel.

81 She is not present in the *Shu ching* at all. In early texts she also appears as Nü Wa and Nü Hsi. Maspero (1924), 52-55.

82 Schafer (1967b), 255.

83 Rotours (1966), 262.

84 LH, "Shun ku."

85 "Ta huang hsi ching."

86 "Hai nei pei ching."

87 Schafer (1951), 156, based on Ch'en Meng-chia.

88 Hastings (1962), XI, 410.

89 Eberhard (1968), 115, places them among his Yao and Thai cultures.

90 *Hua wan wu.* Cf. *tsao hua, tsao wu che.* SWCT, ch. 12.

91 See the Li Po quotation on p. 72.

92 See, for instance, *Li chi*, "Ming t'ang wei."

93 Maspero (1924), 74-75; Schafer (1967b), 13.

94 Graves (1958), 517.

95 Wen (1935), 841, 855-858.

96 Kuo Mo-jo via Eberhard (1968), 85-86.

97 Eberhard (1968), 122-123, 139-141, 399-400, names and describes many water goddesses at the level of popular lore and cult. Some are transformed shamankas and protectresses of seafarers, often with erotic traits in their cults. In many cases they appear to have originally been non-Chinese spirits, that is, goddesses of the Miao and the Thai assimilated to the dominant culture.

98 Maspero (1950), 205, 211.

99 Rousselle (1941), 141-143; paraphrased in Schafer (1967b), 80.

100 Hastings (1962), XI, 403.

101 Hastings (1962), XII, 709.

102 Hastings (1962), XII, 711.

103 Graves (1958), 158-159, 438-439.

104 Wen (1935), 842; Kaltenmark (1935), 101. Wen I-to has also remarked that in a variant text of the *Kao t'ang fu* she is called "youngest daughter of the deity" *(ti chih chi*

*nü)* and is therefore identical with the nubile girl of the *Ts'ao feng* in the *Shih ching*.

105 That is, near Tan-yang. Sun (1936), 1002.

106 Li Tuan, "Wu shan kao," CTS, 285, 3242. The same number is found repeatedly in other T'ang poems.

107 These are from the enumeration in the TuSCC, "Shan ch'uan tien," ch. 177, ts'e 197, p. 32b.

108 Some authorities believe that it is Sung Yü rather than the king who is visited by the goddess. It is impossible to be sure, because the written characters for "king" and "jade" were identical in the ancient script, although in the modern script the latter has been distinguished by the addition of a dot. Even Shen Kua, in Sung times, thought that editorial alterations had substituted the king for the poet. This view is supported by the modern translator of the *Shen nü fu*. See Erkes (1928), 388. By T'ang times, at any rate, it was universally assumed that it was the king who became the lover of the goddess.

109 Wen (1935), 844-845, 847-849. She is especially visible in the odes of Ts'ao *(Ts'ao feng, Hou jen)*.

110 Wen (1935), 851, quoting *Shih ming*.

111 See Hawkes (1962), 37-39, 185, and Hawkes (1967), 73-74 and *passim*. Both poems are translated in the former. The latter gives a "greatly altered" translation of one of them, the *Hsiang chün*. Both are translated in Waley (1956), 29-30, 33-36.

112 Hawkes (1967), 72-73.

113 Hawkes (1967), 72.

114 Hawkes (1962), 35-36; Hawkes (1967), 77.

115 Schwarz (1967), 446-447.

116 This doctrine was first stated explicitly in Liu Hsiang's euhemerizing LiNC, 1, 1b-2b. In SHC, however, Fairy Radiance is treated as an entirely different personage from the daughters of the god. See "Ta huang nan ching," at Pu-t'ing chih shan. The goddess, singular or plural, had other titles elsewhere; for example, she is

"Hsiang Fairy" *(Hsiang o)* in Chang Heng's "Hsi ching fu" (WH, 2, 19a), and "Hsiang Consort" in Mu Hsüan-hsü, "Chiang fu" (WH, 12, 14a). Liu Ch'ang-ch'ing, "Hsiang fei shih, hsü," CTW, 346, 10a-10b, notes that the *Ch'in ts'ao,* a book of poetry attributed to Ts'ai Yung of the Han period, contained songs titled "Complaint of the Hsiang Consort" and "Song of the Lady of the Hsiang."

117  Liu Ch'ang-ch'ing, *loc. cit.* For modern summaries, see Fujino (1951), 140-144; Waley (1956), 31-35; Wen (1961), 63-64; Eberhard (1968), 37-38.

118  Kuo Mo-jo, cited in Eberhard (1968), 37-38.

119  Waley (1956), 14-15, emphasizes the characteristic transience of the shaman's affair with the deity in China as contrasted with Siberia.

120  See Eberhard (1968), 40, for "mountain ghosts" as goddesses. Sun (1936), 978-979, 998-999, pronounces definitely on the identity of the two goddesses. Waley (1956), 53-56, treats the Mountain Spirit as male, but admits that it could be as easily treated as female.

121  For the latter, see Eberhard (1968), 38.

122  Hawkes (1967), 82.

123  Hawkes, (1967), 91.

124  Schafer (1967b), 121.

125  Hawkes (1967), 93. Hawkes detects other elements in the late *fu* of Szu-ma Hsiang-ju, Pan Ku and Chang Heng, especially the rhetorical devices of the pre-Han sophists. See Hawkes (1967), 89. There is good support in the accepted modern interpretations of shamanism for the connections between trance language and poetic language. See, for example, Eliade (1964), 510-511, where he writes of the relationship between poetry and inspired shamanistic utterances and secret and allegorical languages—the creations equally of poet and shaman.

126  Campbell (1961), is dedicated to the study of the many

manifestations of this subject. See also Eliade (1964), 73-78, for many examples of Siberian shamans with celestial wives.

CHAPTER 2

1   Schafer (1962), 295-296.

2   Schafer (1963d), 204, 206.

3   Hsüan Tsung, "Ch'ien kuan chi wu yüeh szu tu fen ho yü shih chao," CTW, 29, 14b-15b.

4   Hsüan Tsung, "Ch'ien kuan ch'i yü chao," CTW, 28, 5a-5b.

5   Schafer (1962), 295.

6   Sun Ti, "Sheng feng po yü shih wei chung szu ch'ih," CTW, 310, 15b-16a.

7   Chang Yüeh, "Sai chiang wen," CTW, 233, 10a-10b.

8   Schafer (1963d), 205. Han Yü's ode in praise of this deity identified it with the ancient smith god of the south, Chu Jung.

9   Schafer (1951), 142 n. 33, from YYTT, 14, 6b.

10   Kaltenmark (1953), 101. Kaltenmark notes a particular example in Chang Heng's *Nan tu fu* "Rhapsody on the Metropolis of the South."

11   Ch'u Szu-tsung, "Sheng nü tz'u," CTS, 594, 6888.

12   Ts'en Shen, "Lung nü tz'u," CTS, 198, 2044.

13   Rotours (1966), 262, with picture from A. Stein, *Innermost Asia* (Oxford, 1928), III, pl. 109.

14   See, for instance, the large number of such places listed in YTCS, *passim.*

15   SIC, b, 14b, YTCS, 32, 12b-13a.

16   TS, 40, 4b.

17   Ch'iao T'an, "Nü Kua ling chi," CTW, 451, 11b-13a.

18   TS, 35, 6a.

19   YYTT, 1, 3; also in TPKC, 304, 1b.

20   CTS, 570, 6613.

21  Liu Ts'ang, "T'i Wu shan miao," CTS, 586, 6794.
22  Wen T'ing-yün, "Wu shan shen nü miao," CTS, 581, 6737.
23  Liu Yü-hsi, "Wu shan shen nü miao," CTS, 361, 4082.
24  CSCN, a, 1.
25  In *Ch'u tz'u,* *"Chiu t'an."*
26  See Eberhard (1968), 40, for the early references to her.
27  Hawkes (1961), 321.
28  The imitation of the language of the first part of this question in the much later *Lo shen chuan* and its significance will be taken note of below.
29  Ultimately a Han description from Szu-ma Piao, *Hsü Han shu.*
30  "Lo shen fu," WH, 19, 15a-20b.
31  LTMHC, 5, 170.
32  SC, 28, 0115b. The text refers to the Mien River, a name for the upper reach of the Han near its source in Shensi. The time was the reign of Ch'in Shih Huang Ti. Li Shan's commentary on the *Chiang fu* of Kuo P'u (*Wen hsüan,* ch. 12) mentions a man who encounters two mysterious women who might be regarded as a pair of Han River goddesses, comparable to the regularly twinned goddesses of the Hsiang.
33  Yang Hsiung, "Yü lieh fu," WH, 8, 30a.
34  Tso Szu, "Shu tu fu," WH, 4, 29b.
35  Chiang Yen, "Shui shang shen nü fu," CWTWC, 1, 7a.
36  Chiang Yen, "Li se fu," CWTWC, 2, 8b.
37  TS, 4, 3b.
38  SHC as quoted in YTCS, 69, 4b, Cf. YYFTC, 3a. "Nine Rivers" is the Kiukiang of our modern maps, now a town further down the river by Lake P'o-yang.
39  YYFTC, 4a.
40  SIC, a, 8a.
41  YTCS, 69, 4a.
42  YTCS, 69, 4b, quoting the early Sung work *Yüeh-yang lou chi* by Fan Chung-yen.

43  YTCS, 69, 3b, citing *Ch'u ti chi.*

44  Fujino (1951), 144.

45  TPHYC, quoting *Yüan ho chün hsien chih*, 113, 2a-2b, and YTCS, 69, 3a, citing the same source.

46  SHC, "Chung shan ching," 5, 42a-42b.

47  TPHYC, 113, 2a, citing the *Han shu*, "Ti li chih."

48  TS, 41, 9b.

49  TPHYC, 113, 2a.

50  TPHYC, 113, 5a.

51  TPHYC, 113, 8b, for Yüan-chiang *hsien.*

52  Possibly this is the same divine creature who figures in the story of Tu Lan-hsiang, taken from the *Yung ch'eng hsien lu* for inclusion in the TPKC, 62, 4a-4b. There she is an exiled sylph found by a fisherman and raised to beautiful but mysterious maidenhood, when she is summoned back to heaven. This "Orchid Fragrance" cast in conventional Taoist style bears little resemblance to Li Ho's fanciful vision.

53  LCCKS, 4, 155-156; Frodsham (1970), 222.

54  CTS, 864, 9774-9775.

55  Tu Fu, "Hsiang fu jen tz'u" *Concordance,* 544.

56  Liu Ch'ang-ch'ing, "Hsiang fei miao," CTS, 148, 1519.

57  Kao P'ien, "Hsiang fei miao," CTS, 598, 6919.

58  YTCS, 69, 11a.

59  SCC, 38, 4a.

60  Li Ch'ün-yü, "Huang ling miao," CTS, 569, 6603.

61  Li Ch'ün-yü, "Hsiang-yin Chiang t'ing ch'üeh chi yu jen," CTS, 569, 6597.

62  Han Yü, "Chi Hsiang chün fu jen wen," CTW, 568, 1a-1b. Cf. Mori (1969), 247.

63  Han Yü, "Huang ling miao pei," CTW, 561, 10b-12a.

64  TPHYC, 113, 2b; YTCS, 69, 6b.

65  YYFTC, 10b-11a.

66  CTS, 648, 7505.

67  TPHYC, 113, 2b-3a.

68  TPHYC, 113, 5b, with quotation from SHC.

69  TPHYC, 113, 3a.

70 Li Mi-szu, "Hsiang chün miao chi," CTW, 802, 9a-11a.

71 See Schafer (1967b), 26 for the shrines in Kuei-chou.

72 SC, 1, 0006d.

73 Wen (1961), 64-65, rejects finally the idea that the Hsiang goddess has anything to do with the wives of Shun. Hawkes (1967), 76, thinks that the legend of the river goddesses could well have been older in this region than the story of Shun, which may then have been super-imposed on it.

74 See Huang-fu Mi (3 cent. A.D.), commentary on *Li chi* "T'an kung."

75 It is found in the *Li chi,* the *Shan hai ching,* and the *Shih chi.*

76 *Yüan ho chün kuo chih,* quoted in TuSCC, "Shan ch'uan tien," ch. 169.

77 See, for example, Schafer (1967b), 179.

78 Li Ch'i, "Erh fei miao sung P'ei shih yü shih Kuei-yang," CTS, 134, 1365.

79 Liu Tsung-yüan, "Hsiang yüan erh fei miao pei," CTW, 587, 7a-8a. Like Han Yü, Liu Tsung-yüan wrote a num-ber of religious dedications.

80 Li Ch'üan-yü, "Kuei-chou ching chia jen ku chü," CTS, 570, 6605.

81 Chang Mi, "Wan tz'u Hsiang-yüan hsien," CTS, 742, 8451.

82 YTCS, 56, 10b.

83 YTCS, 58, 9b; 70, 8a. The first was named "Temple of Fairy Radiance"; the second was "Temple of the Divine Woman," explained in the note as referring to "the two daughters of the god."

CHAPTER 3

1 Liu Ling-hsien, "Ta wai, erh shou," CLS, 13, 19a-19b.

2 Ming yüeh t'an lung nü, "Yü Ho Kuang-yüan tseng ta shih," CTS, 864, 9775-9776.

3   Li Po, "Shang yün yüeh," LTPWC, 3, 9a.

4   Ch'in T'ao-yü, untitled couplet, CTS, 670, 7663.

5   Chang Tzu-jung, "Wu shan." CTS, 116, 1178.

6   Eberhard (1968), 334.

7   Li Ho, "Wu shan kao," LCCKS, 3, 141-142. Translated in Frodsham (1970), 196.

8   Anderson (1967), 294-295.

9   Schafer (1967b), 42

10  George Santayana, "The Elements and Function of Poetry," in Santayana (1957), 276.

11  Su Cheng, "Wu shan," CTS, 718, 8249.

12  Lu Chao-lin, "Wu shan kao," CTS 42, 522.

13  Tu Fu, "T'ien ch'ih," *Concordance,* 511.

14  Li Hsien-yung, "Wu shan kao," CTS, 644, 7379.

15  Chang Hsüan-chih, "Wu shan kao," CTS, 99, 1065.

16  Shen Ch'üan-ch'i, "Wu shan kao," CTS, 96, 1032.

17  Li Chiao, "Yü," CTS, 59, 701.

18  See Schafer (1967b), 83-86.

19  Li Hsün, "Wu shan i tuan yün," CTS, 896, 10121. Ou-yang Chiung, whose topical and stylistic endeavors were much like those of Li Hsüan, also wrote to this tune. Two stanzas survive in CTS, 896, 10125.

20  Not necessarily a reliable guide, TuSCC, "Shan ch'uan tien," preserves five of his, more than any other single poet quoted.

21  Li Po, "Kan hsing," LTPWC, 22, 4a.

22  Yü Fen, "Wu shan kao," CTS, 599, 6930.

23  Meng Chiao, "Wu shan kao, erh shou," CTS, 372, 4183.

24  In Schafer (1963b), 161, and Frodsham (1970), 213. The poem is Li Ho, "Shen hsien," LCCKS, 4, 151-152.

25  Translated in Frodsham (1970), 214. The poem is Li Ho, "Shen hsien pieh ch'ü," LCCKS, 4, 152.

26  Li Po, "Ku feng, wu, shih chiu shou," LTPWC, 2, 10b.

27  Chang Chiu-ling, "Wu shan kao," CTC, 47, 565.

28  Li P'in, "Kuo wu hsia," CTS, 587, 6819.

29   Ch'i-chi, "Wu shan kao," CTS, 847, 9586.

30   Yen Li-pen, "Wu shan kao," CTS, 39, 503.

31   Ch'üan Te-yü, "Tseng yu jen," CTS, 328, 3674.

32   Li Shang-yin, "Hsi shang tso," CTS, 539, 6167.

33   CY, 273, 7b.

34   As in Lo Ch'iu, PHES, 81:47b.

35   Lo Ch'iu, PHES, 67:45a.

36   Schafer (1963b), 55-56.

37   Wang Ch'i, "Shen nü pu kuo kuan t'an fu," CTW, 769,
     7a-8a.

38   Yen Ching-ai, "T'i Hao-chou Kao-t'ang kuan," CTS,
     871, 9875.

39   Li Chiao, "Lo," CTS, 59, 703.

40   As for instance in Li Po, "Kan hsing, pa shou," no. 2,
     LTPWC, 22, 4b; Li Chiao, "Su," CTS, 60, 712; Liu
     Ts'ang, "Lo shen yüan," CTS, 586, 6799; Wen T'ing-
     yün. "Lien hua," CTS, 583, 6761.

41   T'ang Yen-ch'ien, "Lo shen," CTS, 672, 6785.

42   Li Shang-yin, "Wa," CTS, 539, 6179.

43   Lo Ch'iu, PHES, 36b.

44   Meng Hao-jan, "Ho Chang Erh tzu Jan-hsien huan t'u
     chung yü hsüeh," CTS, 160, 1632.

45   Wang Ch'i, "Ch'ü chiang ch'ih fu," CTW, 770, 20a-21a.

46   Ch'üan Te-yü, "Tsa hsing, wu shou," CTS, 328, 3675.

47   SYTC, 84b.

48   Tu Fu, "Mei p'o hsing," *Concordance*, 28.

49   Tu Fu, "Tz'u nan hsi wang," *Concordance*, 544.

50   Wang Po, "Ts'ai lien fu," CTW, 177, 12a-16a.

51   Li Ch'ün-yü, "Lin shui ch'iang-wei," CTS, 569, 6591.

52   Ku K'uang, "Lung kung ts'ao," CTS, 265, 2941.

53   Chü-yüeh, CCPL, 35.

54   TS, 23b, 7b

55   Meng Chiao, "Hsiao fei yüan," CTS, 372, 4183, trans-
     lated in Graham (1965), 66. He also wrote to "Wu shan
     ch'ü," "Wu shan kao," and "Ch'u yüan." It was sug-
     gested to me by a former student, David Pollack, that

bamboos are immortality symbols, with their persistent root systems and fantastic regenerative powers.

56 Ch'en Yü, "Hsiang fei yüan," CTS, 348, 3894. The other is to be found in CTS, 348, 3889.

57 Hsü Hun, "Chin Li chi shih chiu chü," CTS, 536, 6118.

58 Sung Chih-wen, "Tung-t'ing hu," CTS, 51, 621.

59 Tu Fu, "Su ta shih yü ... Su chih i," *Concordance*, 237-238.

60 Yüan Chen, "Feng ho Tou Jung-chou," CTS, 413, 4578.

61 Li Ho, "Huang t'ou lang," LCCKS, 2, 68. Translated in Frodsham (1970), 68.

62 Su Ti, "Hsüan lung t'uan," CTS, 118, 1192.

63 TuSCC, "Shan ch'uan tien," 298.

64 Chu Ch'ing-yü, "Yü P'ang Fu-yen hsi chiu wang Tung-t'ing," CTS, 515, 5885.

65 Li Ch'ün-yü, "Hsiang chung ku ch'ou, san shou," no. 3, CTS, 568, 6572.

66 Liu Yü-hsi, "Ch'ing Hsiang tz'u, erh shou," no. 1, CTS, 356, 4009.

67 Hu Tseng, "Hsiang ch'uan," CTS, 647, 7420.

68 Wu Jung, "Yü kou shih liu yün," CTS, 685, 7866.

69 Tu Fu, "Feng hsien Liu shao fu hsin hua shan shui chang ko," *Concordance*, 64.

70 Tu Mu, "Pan chu t'ung tien," CTS, 524, 5990.

71 Wen T'ing-yün, "Se-se ch'ai," CTS, 583, 6762.

72 P'i Jih-hsiu, "Shih liu ko," CTS, 611, 7055.

73 P'i Jih-hsiu, "Fou p'ing," CTS, 615, 7095.

74 Li Hsien-yung, "Hsieh seng chi ch'a," CTS, 644, 7387.

75 Li Po, "Wang fu shih," CTS, 185, 1889; Wu Yüan-heng, "Wang fu shih," CTS, 316, 3546.

76 Hsiang chung nü tzu, "I lou yung sung," CTS, 866, 9804.

77 Li Ho, "Chia lung yin ko," LCCKS, *wai chi*, 173-174.

78 Schafer (1963a), 204.

79 Eliade (1964), 448, based on Chavannes (1895), I, 74, n. 3, ultimately from LiNC.

80 Li Po, "Yüan pieh li," LTPWC, 3, 1a.
81 Li Po, "P'ei tsu shu ... yu Tung-t'ing," LTPWC, 18, 6b-7a.
82 The tradition was that Ch'ü Yüan himself had refined such barbarous chants as these in the literary language. Liu Yü-hsi had attempted the same thing during his residence in the southern provinces. Cf. Schafer (1967b), 42.
83 Misinterpreted as "pepper" in Hawkes (1962), 37. A common substitution: pepper from southeast Asia was called by the Chinese "foreign fagara" *(hu chiao)*, but this was not the important native spice used in the scented rites of Chou times and later.
84 Li Chia-yu, "Yeh wen Chiang-nan jen chia . . . chi shih," CTS, 206, 2144.
85 Ku K'uang, "Chu chih ch'ü," CTS, 267, 2970.
86 Li Ch'ün-yü, "Hsiang-yin Chiang t'ing ch'üeh chi yu jen," CTS, 569, 6597. This is referred to above on pp. 79-80.
87 TSCS, 30, 13a.
88 "'Prince T'eng's Gallery': A New Interpretation," in "Notes on T'ang Culture, III," *Monumenta Serica*, 30 (1972-73), 108-116.
89 Yang Chiung, "Wu hsia," CTS, 50, 611.
90 Liu Ch'ang-ch'ing, "Hsiang fei," CTS, 147, 1480.
91 Ma Huai-su, "Feng ho sung Chin-ch'eng Kung chu shih, Hsi-fan Ying chih," CTS, han 2, ts'e 5, 7a.


CHAPTER 4

1 For a start, I recommend Chu (1970) to the reader.
2 Cf. Frodsham (1970), xlv: ". . . traditional commentators, especially Confucian rationalists like the Ch'ing commentator Wang Ch'i, have gone so wildly astray at times in interpreting Ho's work, since they understood neither his mystical temperament nor his patriotism."

3   Chu (1970), 29-30.

4   See Arai (1959), 5-6.

5   "Shen hsien ko," and "Shen hsien pieh ch'ü."

6   Notably the class called *Ch'ing shang ch'ü.* In this class
    fall also such well known forms as "Yü shu hou t'ing
    hua," and "Ch'un chiang hua yüeh yeh," which inspired
    Ch'en Hou chu and Sui Yang Ti respectively. See Wang
    (1955), 167-170; Chu (1970), 9-10.

7   I owe the idea that Li Ho might be considered to be a
    kind of shaman who expressed his ecstasy in poetry
    rather than in trance to J. D. Frodsham, who expressed
    it at a meeting of the Colloquium Orientologicum at the
    University of California (Berkeley) in February of 1969.
    In Frodsham (1970), xxxviii, he offers the same concep-
    tion.

8   *Aşık.* I owe this apt analogy to Phyllis Brooks.

9   Hawkes (1961), 322-323. Li Ho's interest in the super-
    natural world was not restricted to the poems men-
    tioned or translated here. The consorts of Shun, the
    "White Silk Woman" *(su nü),* and Nü Kua all appear as
    fairy musicians in "Li P'ing k'ung-hou yin"; he is not
    indifferent to Hsi Wang Mu ("Yao hua yüeh"); such al-
    most forgotten primordial gods as Ling Lun and
    Hsüan-yüan and their archaic music are resurrected in
    his verses. For examples, see Hawkes (1961), 323-334
    and Arai (1959), 50, 55, 60, 131, 144.

10  Pulleyblank (1968).

11  As reported by Tu Mu. See LCCKS, preface, xii.

12  Li Ho, "Hsiang fei," LCCKS, 1, 60; Frodsham (1970),
    58.

13  Li Ho, "Ti tzu ko," LCCKS, 1, 56; Frodsham (1970), 50.

14  YFSC, 47, 6a.

15  Li Ho, "Li P'ing k'ung-hou yin," LCCKS, 1, 35-36;
    Frodsham (1970), 10-11.

16  Darwin (1795), 117.

17  William Blake, "Visions of the Daughters of Albion."

18 *Chuang tzu* as translated in Schafer (1967a), 63.

19 Li Po, "Tu T'ai shan, liu shou," LTPWC, 17, 8a.

20 Schafer (1963c), 101. See this article throughout for other similar material.

21 Li Ho, "Pei kung fu jen," LCCKS, 4, 155; Frodsham (1970), 221.

22 See Schafer (1963b), 288, n.251, for more on this bird. See also Frodsham (1970), 221.

23 Li Ho, "Lo chu chu chen chu," LCCKS, 1, 58; Frodsham (1970), 54.

24 Arai (1959).


CHAPTER 5

1 Eberhard (1968), 40, regards these cults as particularly connected with the south, and ultimately with the sea-coast and its sea goddesses.

2 SIL, in TPKC, 291, 2b. Cf. Eberhard (1968), 33, 37 ff., for more than one version of this tale.

2 HWC, in TPKC, 295, 1b.

4 HSC, in TPKC, 467, 5b-6b.

5 CTL, in TPKC, 424, 2b.

6 IS, in TPKC, 420, 4a.

7 Liu Tsung-yüan, "Che lung shuo," CTW, 584, 17a-17b.

8 The theme of the outcast goddess is, of course, by no means restricted to water goddesses and dragon women. An example is the story of Tu Lan-hsiang in YHHL (TPKC, 62, 4a-4b). Here a fisherman finds a baby girl crying on the shore of Lake Tung-t'ing. He takes her home and looks after her. She becomes a lovely but somewhat strange young woman. Finally she reveals to her foster parent that she is a "transcendent woman" *(hsien nü)* condemned for a transgression. Her time is up, and she vanishes.

9 YYTT, 10, 78.

10  Eberhard (1937), 64-71.
11  HHKL. The story is reproduced in TPKC, 421, 1b-3b as "Liu Kuan-tz'u." See also the discussion of the tale in Uchida (1955), 119-121.
12  HKL.
13  SIC, a, 4a.
14  Schafer (1967b), 220.
15  IY, in TPKC, 469, 4a.
16  IWC, in TPKC, 298, 4a-4b.
17  PMSY, in TPKC, 425, 4b-5a. This motif goes back at least to the SSC. Cf. a story from that source in TPKC, 468, 3b, which tells of a man who makes love to a beautiful woman in a boat. She turns into an alligator and tries to drag him away. He is lucky enough to escape.
18  TYC, in TPKC, 425, 7b.
19  "Kan huai shih," CTS, 864, 9773; author given as *lung nü* ("a dragon woman").
20  PWC, in TPKC, 291, 1b-2a. The received versions apparently incorporate much post-third-century material.
21  PCCKL, in TPKC, 296, 3b-4a.
22  KIC, in TPKC, 402, 4a-4b.
23  Uchida (1955), 138-139, suspects Indian influence in this and similar tales about dragons and treasures. He is probably right.
24  CSL, in TPKC, 314, 3b.
25  Mandarin *She-mo She-li.*
26  YYTT, in TPKC, 480, 6a-6b.
27  YYTT, 14, 105. Translated in Waley (1952), 171, as "The King of Persia's Daughter."
28  CIC, in TPKC, 309, 1a-5a.
29  Examples in Eberhard (1937), 59-61, with a prototype from SSC.
30  CIC, in TPKC, 471, 1a-1b.
31  PCCKL, in TPKC, 296, 2b-3b.
32  SaHC, in TPKC, 469, 2a-2b. The date and author of this book are unknown. Presumably it is T'ang or pre-T'ang.

33  PCCKL, in TPKC, 396, 8b.
34  "Lo shen chuan," in LNC (TTTS, 14, 63a-73a). Our story occupies pages 66a-69b.
35  Lei Hua, son of Lei Huan.
36  The complete story is given in Chapin (1940). The author notes that there are nine extant versions, of which Miss Chapin herself translated seven, in pp. 2-24. Lei Huan, magistrate of Feng-ch'eng, acting on instructions from the high official Chang Hua, dug up a pair of magic swords with *yin-yang* affinity. They were in a stone case. Chang wore one, Lei the other. Chang's sword disappeared after his execution. Lei Hua let his father's sword fall into Yen-p'ing Ford. He sent a diver to look for it, and he found two dragons sporting there—they were the two swords, mysteriously reunited. These are the Mo-hsieh and Kan-chiang swords, well known from ancient folk tale, assimilated to a supposedly historical episode.
37  That is, in "Five Element" theory, in which the dragon is the sacred animal of the east, of springtime, and of growing things. This contradicts the older and more popular association of the dragon with water, and hence with women.
38  Compare our legend of the barnacle goose.
39  *Ch'en.*
40  That is, Chang Hua.
41  Ma-shih is used both for "horse doctor" and as a double surname. The tale is in the *Lieh hsien chuan.*
42  A translation of "nirvana."
43  Kaltenmark (1953), 101. Kaltenmark quite reasonably equates them with the Han goddess.
44  LHC, 10b-11b. Cf. Kaltenmark (1953), 99-100, where the story is related to the usual legend of drowned women.
45  LHC, in TPKC, 59, 3a-3b.
46  Kaltenmark (1953) suggests that the two gems represent the sun and the moon, and that the goddesses are there-

fore Hsi-ho the sun goddess and Ch'ang-hsi (i.e., Ch'ang-o) the moon goddess. Possibly.

47   *K'ai cheng,* a reign of Wen Tsung.

48   HSC, in TPKC, 310, 5b-6a.

49   IS, in TPKC, 305, 4b-5a.

50   YHYI, in TPKC, 498, 5a-5b.

51   I have followed the version of the text reproduced in TSCCC, pp. 131-132. There is an inferior and corrupt version in TTTS, 9, 1a-2b. The latter is quite unintelligible in places but occasionally suggestive. For instance, where the better text has the dragon woman (discovered under a bridge) veil her face with her sleeve as demanded by maidenly convention, the worse text has her "cover her nakedness." The graphs for *tan* "nakedness" and *hsiu* "sleeve" are very similar.

52   Interested readers will find a short account of this tale, giving the text of Far Floater's farewell song, in YYFTC, 9a.

53   There are many extant editions. I have used the text of Wang (1932). It has been translated as "The Dragon King's Daughter," which gives its name in turn to the anthology *The Dragon King's Daughter* (see *Dragon King* in the bibliography). Uchida (1955) has made a thorough study of the tale. He discovers a germinal ancestor in the *Sou shen chi,* and various later cognates. It has had a strong influence on Sung literature, and an even greater one on Yüan drama. Uchida notes the conjunction of four ancient folklore traits in this story: the message delivered to a water spirit; the visit to an underwater palace; the dragon girl; the final reward.

## CONCLUSION

1   Cf. Northrop Frye, "It is part of the critic's business to show how all literary genres are derived from the quest-myth . . ." Frye (1963), 17.

# Bibliography

PRIMARY SOURCES

*Parenthetical abbreviations stand for books listed under "Collectanea, Encyclopedias and Anthologies," or "Secondary Sources" in the bibliography. They represent the editor or sources used in footnote documentation, unless otherwise stated in the note.*

| | |
|---|---|
| CCPL | Chü-yüeh 居月, *Ch'in ch'ü p'u lu* 琴曲譜錄 (WCHS) |
| ChTS | *Chiu T'ang shu* 舊唐書 (SPPY) |
| CIC | Hsüeh Yung-jo 薛用弱, *Chi i chi* 集異記 (TPKC) |
| CS | *Chin shu* 晉書 (ESWS) |
| CSCN | *Chu shu chi nien* 竹書紀年 (TSCC) |
| CSL | Hsü Hsüan 徐鉉, *Chi shen lu* 稽神錄 (TPKC) |
| CTL | K'ang P'ien 康駢, *Chü t'an lu* 劇談錄 (TPKC) |
| CWTWC | Chiang Yen 江淹, *Liang Chiang Wen-t'ung wen chi* 梁江文通文集 |
| CY | Wang Ting-pao 王定保, *Chih yen* 摭言 (TPKC) |
| HCYT | Shen Ya-chih 沈亞之, *Hsiang chung yüan tz'u* 湘中怨辭 (TSCCC) |
| HHHP | *Hsüan ho hua p'u* 宣和畫譜 (TSCC) |
| HHKL | Li Fu-yen 李復言, *Hsü hsüan kuai lu* 續玄怪錄 (TPKC) |
| HHSP | *Hsüan ho shu p'u* 宣和書譜 (TSCC) |
| HKL | Niu Seng-ju 牛僧孺, *Hsüan kuai lu* 玄怪錄 |

| | |
|---|---|
| HSC | Chang Tu 張讀, *Hsüan shih chih* 宣室志 (TPKC) |
| HWC | Cheng Sui 鄭遂, *Hsia wen chi* 洽聞記 (TPKC) |
| IS | Lu shih 盧氏, *I shih* 逸史 (TPKC) |
| IY | Liu Ching-shu 劉敬叔, *I yüan* 異苑 (TPKC) |
| KIC | Tai Fu 戴孚, *Kuang i chi* 廣異記 (TPKC) |
| KY | *Kuo yü* 國語 (KHCPTS) |
| LCCKS | Li Ho 李賀, *Li Ch'ang-chi ko shih* 李長吉歌詩 (Yang [1964]) |
| LH | Wang Ch'ung 王充, *Lun heng* 論衡 (KHCPTS) |
| LHC | Ko Hung 葛洪, *Lieh hsien chuang* 列仙傳 (KCIS) |
| LIC | Li Ch'ao-wei 李朝威, *Liu I chuan* 柳毅傳 (Wang [1932]) |
| LiNC | Liu Hsiang 劉向, *Lieh nü chuan* 列女傳 (SPTK) |
| LNC | Hsieh Ying 薛瑩, *Lung nü chuan* 龍女傳 (TTTS) |
| LTMYC | Chang Yen-yüan 張彥遠, *Li tai ming hua chi* 歷代名畫記 (TSCC) |
| LTPWC | Li Po 李白, *Li T'ai-po wen chi* 李太白文集 (Hiraoka [1958]) |
| PCCKL | *Pa ch'ao ch'iung kuai lu* 八朝窮怪錄 (TPKC) |
| PHES | Lo Ch'iu 羅虬, *Pi Hung-erh shih* 比紅兒詩 (TTTS) |
| PMSY | Sun Kuang-hsien 孫光憲, *Pei meng so yen* 北夢瑣言 (*TPKC*) |
| PPT | Ko Hung 葛洪, *Pao p'u tzu* 抱朴子 |
| PTKM | Li shih-chen 李時珍, *Pen ts'ao kang mu* 本草綱目 (Hung pao chai ed.) |
| PWC | Chang Hua 張華, *Po wu chih* 博物志 (TPKC) |
| SC | *Shih chi* 史記 (ESWS) |
| SCC | Li Tao-yüan 酈道元, *Shui ching chu* 水經注 (SPTK) |
| SaHC | *San hsia chi* 三峽記 (TPKC) |
| SHC | *Shan hai ching* 山海經 (SPPY) |
| SIC | Jen Fang 任昉, *Shu i chi* 述異記 (LWPS) |
| SIL | Wang Chia 王嘉, *Shih i lu* 拾遺錄 (TPKC) |
| SSC | Kan Pao 干寶, *Sou shen chi* 搜神記 (TPKC) |
| SWCT | Hsü Shen 許慎, *Shuo wen chieh tzu* 說文解字 |
| SYTC | Yang Kuang 楊廣, *Sui Yang Ti chi* 隋煬帝集 (HWLCC) |

TaCTC    *Tao chia tsa chi* 道家雜記 (TPKC)

TC    *Tso chuan* 左傳

TCMHL    Chu Ching-hsüan 朱景玄, *T'ang ch'ao ming hua lu* 唐朝名畫錄 (MSTS)

TCTC    Szu-ma Kuang 司馬光, *Tzu chih t'ung chien* 資治通鑑 (Tokyo, 1892)

TCTL    Yang Shen 楊慎, *Tan ch'ien tsung lu* 丹鉛總錄 (1588 ed.)

TFSPC    *Tung-fang Shuo pieh chuan* 東方朔別傳 (PTKM)

TPHYC    *T'ai p'ing huan yü chi* 太平寰宇記 (Taipei, 1963)

TS    *T'ang shu* 唐書 (SPPY)

TSCS    Chi Yu-kung 計有功, *T'ang shih chi shih* 唐詩紀事 (SPTK)

TYC    Ch'en Shao 陳邵, *T'ung yu chi* 通幽記 (TPKC)

WS    *Wei shu* 魏書 (ESWS)

YFSC    *Yüeh fu shih chi* 樂府詩集 (SPTK)

YHHL    *Yung hsü hsien lu* 墉壚仙錄 (TPKC)

YHYI    Fan Shu 范攄, *Yün hsi yu i* 雲溪友議 (TPKC)

YTCS    Wang Hsiang-chih 王象之, *Yü ti chi sheng* 輿地紀勝 (1849 ed.)

YYFTC    Fan Chih-ming 范致明, *Yüeh-yang feng t'u chi* 岳陽風土記 (KCIS)

YYTT    Tuan Ch'eng-shih 段成式, *Yu-yang tsa tsu* 酉陽雜俎 (TSCC)

*Collectanea, Encyclopedias and Anthologies*

CHNPCS    *Ch'üan Han San kuo Chin Nan pei ch'ao shih* 全漢三國晉南北朝詩

CLS    *Ch'üan Liang shih* 全梁詩 (CHNPCS)

CTS    *Ch'üan T'ang shih* 全唐詩 (Peking, 1960)

CTW    *Ch'üan T'ang wen* 全唐文

ESWS    *Erh shih wu shih* 二十五史 (K'ai ming ed.)

HWLCC    *Han Wei Liu ch'ao po san chia chi* 漢魏六朝百三家集

KCIS    *Ku chin i shih* 古今逸史

KHCPTS    *Kuo-hsüeh chi-pen ts'ung-shu* 國學基本叢書

LWPS    *Lung wei pi shu* 龍威秘書

| MSTS | *Mei shu ts'ung shu* 美術叢書 |
| SPPY | *Szu pu pei yao* 四部備要 |
| SPTK | *Szu pu ts'ung k'an* 四部叢刊 |
| TPKC | *T'ai p'ing kuang chi* 太平廣記 |
| TSCC | *Ts'ung shu chi ch'eng* 叢書集成 |
| TSCCC | Lu Hsün 魯迅, *T'ang Sung ch'uan ch'i chi* 唐宋傳奇集 (Hong Kong, 1964) |
| TTTS | *T'ang tai ts'ung shu* 唐代叢書 |
| TuSCC | *T'u shu chi ch'eng* 圖書集成 |
| WCHS | *Wu ch'ao hsiao shuo* 五朝小說 |
| WH | *Wen hsüan* 文選 (SPTK) |

## SECONDARY SOURCES

ANDERSON, E. N., JR.
1967 "The Folksongs of the Hong Kong Boat People," *Journal of American Folklore*, 80 (1967), 285-296.

ARAIKEN
1955 "Ri Ga no shi—toku ni sono shikisai ni tsuite," *Chūgoku bungaku hō*, 3 (Kyoto, 1955), 61-90.
1959 *Ri Ga* (Tokyo, 1959).

CAMPBELL, JOSEPH
1961 *The Hero with a Thousand Faces* (Bollingen Series XVII; 3rd printing, New York, 1961).

CARRINGTON, RICHARD
1960 "The Natural History of the Mermaid," *Horizon*, 2/3 (January, 1960), 129-136.

CHAPIN, HELEN B.
1940 *Toward the Study of the Sword as Dynastic Talisman: The Fêng-ch'êng Pair and the Sword of Han Kao Tsu* (unpublished Ph.D. dissertation, University of California, Berkeley, 1940).

CHAVANNES ÉDOUARD
1895 *Les mémoires historiques de Se-ma Ts'ien* (Paris, 1895).

CHOU LANG-FENG

    1926 *Shih-jen Li Ho* (Kuo-hsüeh hsiao ts'ung-shu).

CHU CH'I-FENG

    1934 *Tz'u t'ung* (Shanghai, 1934).

CHU TZU-CH'ING

    1970 *Li Ho nien-p'u* (Hong Kong, 1970).

*Concordance*

    1940 "A Concordance to the Poems of Tu Fu." *Harvard-Yenching Institute Sinological Index Series,* II, Suppl. 14 (Cambridge, 1940).

CORAL-RÉMUSAT, GILBERTE DE

    1936 "Animaux fantastiques de l'Indochine, de l'Insulinde et de la Chine," *Bulletin de l'École Franqise d'Extrême-Orient,* 36 (1936), 427-435.

DARWIN, ERASMUS

    1795 *The Botanic Garden. A Poem, in two parts.* Part I. *Containing The Economy of Vegetation.* Part II. *The Loves of the Plants, with Philosophical Notes* (3rd ed., London, 1795).

DAVIDSON, H. R. ELLIS

    1968 *Gods and Myths of Northern Europe* (Penguin Books, 1968).

*Dragon King*

    1954 *The Dragon King's Daughter; Ten Tang Dynasty Stories* (Peking, 1954).

EBERHARD, W.

    1937 *Typen chinesischer Volksmärchen* (F F Communications No. 120; Helsinki, 1937).

    1942 "Lokalkulturen im alten China," I, *T'oung Pao,* Supplement to Vol. 37 (1942); II, *Monumenta Serica,* Monograph 3 (1942).

    1968 *The Local Cultures of South and East China,* translated from the German by Alide Eberhard (Leiden, 1968).

ELIADE, MIRCEA

    1964 *Shamanism: Archaic Techniques of Ecstasy* (New York, 1964).

ERKES, E.

    1928 "Shen-nü-fu, The Song of the Goddess, by Sung Yüh," *T'oung Pao, 25 (1928), 387-402.*

FRODSHAM, J. D.

    1970 *The Poems of Li Ho (791-817) (Oxford, 1970).*

FRYE, NORTHROP

    1963 *Fables of Identity: Studies in Poetic Mythology* (A Harbinger Book, New York, 1963).

FUJINO IWATOMO

    1951 *Fukei bungaku-ron—Soji o chūshin to shite* [A Study of Literature with the Medium Tradition in Ancient China] (Tokyo, 1951).

GAUTIER, JUDITH

    1901 *Le livre de jade: poésies traduites du chinois* (enlarged edition, Paris, n.d., preface of 1901).

GLUECK, NELSON

    1965 *Deities and Dolphins* (New York, 1965).

GRAHAM, A. C.

    1965 *Poems of the Late T'ang* (Penguin Books, 1965).

GRAVES, ROBERT

    1958 *The White Goddess; A Historical Grammar of Poetic Myth* (New York, 1958)

HASTINGS, JAMES

    1962 *Encyclopedia of Religion and Ethics* (New York, 1962).

HAWKES, DAVID

    1961 "The Supernatural in Chinese Poetry," *The Far East: China and Japan* (University of Toronto Quarterly Supplements No. 5, Toronto, 1961), 311-324.

    1962 *Ch'u Tz'u; The Songs of the South: An Ancient Chinese Anthology* (Beacon Paperback, Boston, 1962).

    1967 "The Quest of the Goddess," *Asia Major, 13 (1967),* 71-94.

HERSHOLT, JEAN

    1942 Andersen's Fairy Tales

HIRAOKA TAKEO

    1958 *Rihaku no sakuhin* (Kyoto, 1958).

IKEDA SUETOSHI

    1953 "Ryūjin kō," *Tōhōgaku,* 6 (June, 1953), 1-7.

KALTENMARK, MAX

    1953 *Le lieh-sien tchouan (Biographies légendaires des Immortels taoïstes de l'antiquité)* (Pékin, 1953).

K'ANG P'EI-CH'U

    1962 "Shuo lung," *Ta-lu tsa-chih,* 25/8 (October 31, 1962), 24-26.

LU K'AN-JU

    1929 *Sung Yü* (Shanghai, 1929).

MAENO NAOAKI

    1963 *Tō Sō denki shū* (2 vols., Tokyo, 1963-1964).

MASPERO, HENRI

    1924 "Légendes mythologiques dans le Chou King," *Journal Asiatique,* 214 (1924), 1-100.

    1950 *Le Taoïsme* (Mélanges posthumes sur les religions et l'histoire de la Chine, II; Paris, 1950).

MORI MIKISABURŌ

    1969 *Chūgoku kodai shinwa* (2nd ed., Tokyo, 1969).

NEEDHAM, JOSEPH

    1954 *Science and Civilisation in China,* I (Cambridge, 1954).

    1970 *Clerks and Craftsmen in China and the West* (Cambridge, 1970).

PLUMMER, CHARLES, AND JOHN EARLE

    1965 *Two of the Saxon Chronicles Parallel,* I (Oxford, 1965).

PULLEYBLANK, E. G.

    1968 "The Rhyming Categories of Li Ho (791-817)," *The Tsing Hua Journal of Chinese Studies,* n.s. 7/1 (August, 1968), 1-22.

ROTOURS, ROBERT DES

1966 "Le culte des cinq dragons sous la dynastie des T'ang (618-907)," *Mélanges de Sinologies offerts à Monsieur Paul Demiéville* (Paris, 1966), 261-280.

ROUSSELLE, ERWIN

1951 "Die Frau in Gesellschaft und Mythos der Chinesen," *Sinica, 16 (1941), 130-151.*

SANTAYANA, GEORGE

1959 Interpretations of Poetry and Religion (New York, 1959).

SCHAFER, E. H.

1951 "Ritual Exposure in Ancient China," *Harvard Journal of Asiatic Studies,* 14 (1951), 130-184.

1954 *The Empire of Min* (Tokyo, 1954).

1956 "The Development of Bathing Customs in Ancient and Medieval China and the History of the Floriate Clear Palace," *Journal of the American Oriental Society,* 76 (1956), 57-82.

1962 "The Conservation of Nature under the T'ang Dynasty," *Journal of the Economic and Social History of the Orient,* 5 (1962), 279-308.

1963a "The Auspices of T'ang," *Journal of the American Oriental Society,* 83 (1963), 197-225.

1963b *The Golden Peaches of Samarkand: A Study of T'ang Exotics* (Berkeley and Los Angeles, 1963).

1963c "Mineral Imagery in the Paradise Poems of Kuanhsiu," *Asia Major,* 10 (1963), 73-102.

1963d "Notes on T'ang Culture," *Monumenta Serica,* 21 (1963), 194-221.

1965 "Notes on T'ang Culture, II," *Monumenta Serica,* 24 (1965), 130-154.

1967a *Ancient China* (with the Editors of Time-Life Books; Great Ages of Man Series; New York, 1967).

1967b *The Vermilion Bird: T'ang Images of the South* (Berkeley and Los Angeles, 1967).

SCHWARZ, ERNST

1967 "Das Drachenbootfest und die 'Neun Lieder'," *Wissenschaftliche Zeitschrift der Humboldt-Universität zu Berlin Gesellschaftsund Sprachwissenschaftliche Reihe,* 16 (1967), 443-452.

SIERKSMA, F.

1966 *Tibet's Terrifying Deities: Sex and Aggression in Acculturation* (Rutland and Tokyo, 1966).

STEIN, R. A.

1935 "Jardins en miniature d'Extrême-Orient," *Bulletin de l'École Française d'Extrme-Orient,* 42 (1942), 1-104.

SUN TSO-YÜN

1936 "Chiu Ko 'Shan kuei' k'ao," *Ch'ing hua hua hsüeh pao,* 11 (1936), 977-1005.

THIEL, JOS.

1968 "Schamanismus im alten China," *Sinologica,* 10 (1968), 149-204.

THOMAS, ELIZABETH M.

1959 *The Harmless People* (Vintage Books, New York, 1959).

UCHIDA MICHIO

1955 "Ryū-Ki-den ni tsuite—suishin setsuwa no tenkai o chūshin ni—." *Tōhoku daigaku bungakubu kenkyū nempō,* 6 (1955), 107-141.

VON ZACH, ERWIN

1958 *Die chinesische Anthologie* (Harvard-Yenching Institute Studies, XVIII, Cambridge, 1958).

WALEY, ARTHUR

1952 *The Real Tripitaka and other Pieces* (London, 1952).

1956 *The Nine Songs: A Study of Shamanism in Ancient China* (2nd impression, London, 1956).

WANG P'I-CHIANG (WANG KUO-YÜAN)

1932 *T'ang-jen hsiao-shuo* (Shanghai, 1932).

WANG YÜN-HSI
   1955 *Liu-ch'ao yüeh-fu yü min-ko* (Shanghai, 1955).

WEN CH'UNG-I
   1960 "Chiu-ko-chung Ho Po chih yen-chiu," *Bulletin of the Institute of Ethnology, Academia Sinica,* 9 (1960), 139-162.

WEN I-TO
   1935 "Kao-t'ang shen-nü shuo chih fen-hsi," *Ch'ing-hua hsüeh-pao,* 10 (1935), 837-865.
   1948 *Wen I-to ch'üan-chi* (Shanghai, 1948).
   1956 *Shen-hua yü shih* (Wen I-to ch'üan-chi hsüan, No. 1, Peking, 1956).

WONG MAN
   1962 "Prologue to 'Prince T'eng's Pavilion'," *Eastern Horizon,* 2/8 (August, 1962), 21-28.

YANG CHIA-LO
   1964 *Li Ho shih chu* (Taipei, 1964).

YANG SHOU-LING
   1904 *Li-tai yü-ti yen-ko hsien-yao t'u* (1904-1911).

# Glossary A

## NAMES OF T'ANG WRITERS

Chang Chiu-ling (673–740)
張九齡

Chang Hsün-chih (late 7th
cent.) 張循之

Chang Mi (fl. 940) 張泌

Chang Tu (fl. 853) 張讀

Chang Tzu-jung (fl. 728)
張子容

Chang Yüeh (667–730) 張說

Ch'en Han (7th cent.) 陳翰

Ch'en Shao (10th cent.) 陳邵

Ch'en Yü (fl. 806) 陳羽

Cheng Sui (T'ang) 鄭澊

Ch'i-chi (fl. 881) 齊己

Ch'iao T'an (fl. 754) 喬潭

Ch'ien Ch'i (fl. 766) 錢起

Ch'in T'ao-yü (fl. 890)
秦韜玉

Chu Ch'ing-yü (fl. 826)
朱慶餘

Ch'u Szu-tsung (fl. 853)
儲嗣宗

Ch'üan Te-yü (759–818)
權德輿

Fan Shu (fl. 877) 范攄

Fang Kan (fl. 860) 方干

Han Yü (768–824) 韓愈

Hsü Hsüan (916–991) 徐鉉

Hsü Hun (fl. 844) 許渾

Hsüeh Ying (fl. 841) 薛瑩

Hu Tseng (fl. 877) 胡曾

K'ang P'ien (fl. 886) 康駢

Kao P'ien (?–887) 高駢

Ku K'uang (ca. 725–ca.
814) 顧況

Lang Shih-yüan (758–815)
郎士元

Li Ch'ao-wei (fl. 759) 李朝威

Li Ch'i (fl. 742) 李頎

Li Chia-yu (fl. 757) 李嘉祐

Li Chiao (644–713) 李嶠

Li Ch'ün-yü (fl. 847) 李羣玉

Li Fu-yen (fl. 831) 李復言

Li Ho (791–817) 李賀

Li Hsien-yung (fl. 873)
李咸用

Li Hsün (fl. 896) 李珣

Li Mi-szu (fl. 860–873)
李密思

Li P'in (fl. 860) 李頻

Li Po (701–762) 李白

Li Shang-yin (813–858) 李商隱

221

# Glossary B

## OTHER NAMES AND TITLES

Chang Heng 張衡
Chang Hua 張華
Ch'ang-hsi 常羲
Ch'ang-o 嫦娥
Chao Tsung 昭宗
Chen 甄
Chiang Yen 江淹
Ch'in ts'ao 琴操
Ch'ing shang ch'ü 清商曲
Chu Jung 祝融
Ch'u tz'u 楚辭
Ch'un chiang hua yüeh yeh 春江花月夜
Chung Tsung 中宗
Chü-yüeh 居月
Ch'ü Yüan 屈原
Fan Li 范蠡
Fang Chung-yen 范仲淹
Feng I 馮夷
Fu fei 宓妃
Heng-o 姮娥
Ho Kuang-yüan 何光遠
Ho po 河伯
Hsi-ho 羲和
Hsi-men Pao 西門豹

Hsiang chün 湘君
Hsiang fu jen 湘夫人
Hsien Tsung 憲宗
Hsüan Tsung 玄宗
Hsüan-yüan 軒轅
Huang-fu Mi 皇甫謐
I 羿
Jama Shali 射摩舍利
Kao-t'ang fu 高唐賦
Ku K'ai-chih 顧凱之
Kuo Hsien 郭憲
Lei Hua 雷華
Lei Huan 雷煥
Lei Man 雷滿
Li Ch'un 李純
Li Chung-mao 李重茂
Li Heng 李亨
Li Hsiao-kung 李孝恭
Li Lung-chi 李隆基
Ling Lun 伶倫
Liu Ch'e 劉徹
Liu Ling-hsien 劉令嫻
Lo shen chuan 洛神傳
Ma Ju-tzu 馬孺子
Ma-shih 馬師

Ming Ti 明帝
Mu Hsüan-hsü 木玄虚
Nü Hsi 女希
Nü Kua 女媧
Nü Wa 女娃
Nü Ying 女英
O Huang 娥皇
Shan kuei 山鬼
Shang Ti 殤帝
Shen Kua 沈适
Shen nü fu 神女賦
Su nü 素女
Su Tsung 肅宗
Szu-ma Piao 司馬彪
Szu-ma Shao 司馬紹
T'ai Tsung 太宗
T'ang Lung 唐隆
Ti Jen-chieh 狄仁傑
Ti tzu 帝子

T'o-pa K'o 拓跋恪
Tou (queen) 竇
Ts'ai Yung 蔡邕
Tso Szu 左思
Tu Hung-erh 杜紅兒
Tu Lan-hsiang 杜蘭香
Tung (shamanka) 董
Wang Chi-p'eng 王繼鵬
Wang Ch'i-han 王齊翰
Wang Ch'ung 王充
Wang Yen-chün 王延鈞
Wei (queen) 韋
Wei Kao 韋皋
Wen I-to 聞一多
Yang Hsiung 楊雄
Yang Kuang 楊廣
Yao Chi 瑤姬
Yü shu hou t'ing hua
    玉樹後庭花

# Glossary C

## PLACE NAMES

Ch'ao-chou 潮州

Chi (river) 濟

Chin-chou 金州

Chiu i shan 九疑山

Chün shan 君山

Han (river) 漢

Hao-chou 濠州

Heng (mountain) 衡

Hsiang (river) 湘

Hsiang-yin 湘陰

Hsiao (river) 瀟

Huai (river) 淮

Hung-chou 洪州

Kan-chou 贛州

Kao-t'ang 高唐

Kiang [Chiang] (river) 江

Kuei-chou 桂州

Kuei-lin 桂林

Kuo-chou 虢州

Li (river in Kwangsi) 灕

Li (river in Hunan) 澧

Li (mountain) 驪

Lien-chou 連州

Ling-ling 零陵

Lo (river) 洛

Mien (river) 沔

Ou (nation) 歐

Pa-ling 巴陵

Pei chu 北渚

P'eng tao 蓬島

Tan-yang 丹陽

Tao-chou 道州

Ts'ang-wu 蒼梧

Wu shan 巫山

Yai (mountain) 崖

Yung-chou 永州

Yüan (river) 沅

Yüan-chiang 沅江

Yüan Chiao 圓嶠

Yüeh-chou 岳州

Yüeh-yang 岳陽

# Glossary D

## WORDS AND PHRASES

che hsien 謫仙

ch'en "clam monster" 蜃

chi "record" 記

chi nü 季女

chiao [*kǎu] "kraken" 蛟

chu "holm" 渚

ch'uan ch'i 傳奇

*ghung "rainbow" 虹

*ghwǎ/wǎ "frog" 蛙

hsi "shaman" 覡

hsiao shuo 小說

hsien "transcendent" 仙

hsiu "sleeve" 袖

hua wan wu 化萬物

ku lung (=Cambodian
    kurung) 古龍

*k'ung-lung "hollowed"
    空窿

*kwǎ (in Nü Kua) 媧

*kwǎ "snail" 蝸

*kwět-lyung "cavity" 窟窿

*k'you-lyong "hill" 丘隴

*kyung "bow" 弓

*kyung "house; [later]
    palace" 宮

*k'yung "vault; dome" 穹

*lung "cage; basket" 籠

*lyong "hillock" 隴

*lyong "mound" 壟

*lyong "rain serpent;
    dragon" 龍

*lyung "arched; prominent"
    隆

*lyung-gyung "arched;
    humped" 隆穹

*ngei "female rainbow" 蜺

p'u "reach" 浦

p'u wu yü jih 暴巫于日

sheng nü 聖女

szu tu 四瀆

tan "nakedness" 袒

ti chih chi nü 帝之季女

ti tzu 帝子

tou (constellation) 斗

tsao hua 造化

tsao wu che 造物者

*wa "covert; hole; hiding
    place" 渦

*wa "dimple; depression;
    water-worn hole" 窩

226

*wa (in Nü Wa, for Nü Kua; dialect word for "a beauty" in Yangtze region) 娃

*wa "still pond; puddle; stagnant water" 洼

wu [*myu] "shamanka" 巫

wu shih 巫師

yüeh fu 樂府

# Index

*Note:* Some words and concepts pervade the book, and indeed constitute its essence. Accordingly they have not been indexed. They are the following: cloud, dew, dryad, erotic, female, goddess, lake, literature, mermaid, mist, myth, nereid, nymph, poetry, rain, river, sea, sex, spring, T'ang, water, woman.

Design by David Bullen
Typeset in Mergenthaler Sabon
by Robert Sibley
Printed by McNaughton-Gunn
on acid-free paper